Al Burt's Florida

The Florida History and Culture Series

Al Burt's

UNIVERSITY PRESS OF FLORIDA

Gainesville
Tallahassee
Tampa
Boca Raton
Pensacola
Orlando
Miami
Jacksonville

Snowbirds, Sand Castles, and Self-Rising Crackers

Al Burt

The Florida History and Culture Series consists of important works devoted to understanding the state's rich history and diversity. Accessible and attractively designed, each book will focus on various topics of historical interest, such as the environment, politics, literature, material culture, and cultural studies.

Florida History and Culture Series
Al Burt, *Al Burt's Florida: Snowbirds, Sand Castles, and Self-Rising Crackers*
Marvin Dunn, *Black Miami in the Twentieth Century*

---

02 01 00 99 98   6 5 4 3

LIBRARY OF CONGRESS CATALOGING-IN-PUBLICATION DATA
Burt, Al.
[Florida]
Al Burt's Florida: snowbirds, sand castles, and self-rising crackers
p. cm.—(The Florida history and culture series)
Includes bibliographical references.
ISBN 0-8130-1542-1 (alk. paper)
1. Florida—History. 2. Florida—Social life and customs.
3. Florida—Description and travel. I. Title. II. Series.
F311.5.B875 1997 97-9454
975.9—dc21

The University Press of Florida is the scholarly publishing agency for the State University System of Florida, comprised of Florida A & M University, Florida Atlantic University, Florida International University, Florida State University, University of Central Florida, University of Florida, University of North Florida, University of South Florida, and University of West Florida.

University Press of Florida
15 Northwest 15th Street
Gainesville, FL 32611

For the good folk of Melrose

Other books by Al Burt:
Becalmed in the Mullet Latitudes
Florida: A Place in the Sun
Papa Doc (with Bernard Diederich)

Contents

Foreword

Al Burt's Florida: Snowbirds, Sand Castles, and Self-Rising Crackers is the inaugural volume of a new series devoted to the study of Florida history and culture. During the past half century, the burgeoning population and increased national and international visibility of Florida have sparked a great deal of popular interest in the state's past, present, and future. As the favorite destination of countless tourists and as the new home for millions of retirees and other migrants, modern Florida has become a demographic, political, and cultural bellwether. But, unfortunately, the quantity and quality of the literature on Florida's distinctive heritage and character have not kept pace with the Sunshine State's enhanced status. In an effort to remedy this situation—to provide an accessible and attractive format for the publication of Florida-related books—the University Press of Florida has established the Florida History and Culture series.

As coeditors of the series, we are committed to the creation of an eclectic but carefully crafted set of books that will provide the field of Florida studies with a new focus and that will encourage Florida researchers and writers to consider the broader implications and context of their work. The series will include standard academic monographs, memoirs, anthologies, and works of synthesis. And, while the series will feature books of historical interest, we encourage authors researching Florida's environment, politics, literature, and popular or material culture to submit their manuscripts for possible inclusion in the series. We want each book to retain a distinct personality and voice, but at the same time we hope to foster a sense of community and collaboration among Florida scholars.

We feel especially fortunate to begin with the publication of *Al Burt's Florida*. Al Burt is a regional treasure, a journalist with the instincts of a detective and the soul of a poet. Born in Georgia but removed to Florida in infancy, he has devoted much of his life to the study of his semi-native state. A graduate of the University of Florida, he spent five years as a reporter with the *Jacksonville Journal* before moving to the *Miami Herald* in 1955. As a city editor, Latin America editor, and editorial writer for the *Herald,* he became a fixture of south Florida journalism and the winner of several national awards for distinguished newspaper writing. But in 1973 his career took a fateful turn when he agreed to become the paper's roving statewide correspondent. Relocating his family in the small north-central Florida town of Melrose, he began to explore the rich diversity of Florida, from panhandle to peninsula, from Pensacola to Key Largo and beyond. For more than twenty years, until his retirement in 1996, he roamed the state as an unofficial journalist laureate. Probing aspects of local and regional life that were beyond the direct experience of most of the state's urban residents, especially newcomers, he produced a steady stream of searching and eloquent commentary on Florida and Floridians.

In 1985, some of Burt's work appeared in a collection titled *Becalmed in the Mullet Latitudes,* but this volume represents the first effort to reshape his writings and reflections into a work of synthesis. Mixing autobiography, folklore, and historical analysis, he offers us *his* Florida, which in a real sense turns out to be *our* Florida. Though intensely personal, his portrait of the state combines history and homespun philosophy, elemental specificity and a search for transcendent truths, a strong sense of place, and an appreciation for the disruptive power of change. Pointed yet colorfully rendered, his evocative prose ranks with the best of American regional writing. In the tradition of the WPA state guides and the Rivers of America series, *Al Burt's Florida* is an artful example of folk history, a product of literary imagination and historical sensibility. Readers seeking an understanding of Florida's historical and cultural development will find much in this remarkable volume to enjoy and ponder.

Raymond Arsenault and Gary R. Mormino
Series Editors

Preface

Nearly a quarter century of exploring Florida generates more than just memories. A personal sense of history takes shape. This memoir recalls some of the impressions formed during two decades when I traveled the entire state, from Key West to Pensacola to Fernandina Beach and back down to Miami, stopping at cities and villages along the way and searching for clues about a changing Florida among as many people and situations as I could reach. It has a center: my lakeside home near the historic village of Melrose. That was important. For any steady look at nomadic Florida, where tidal movements and migrations affect all, an anchor is needed.

The book relies both on material used in speeches around the state and on that gathered as a columnist for *The Miami Herald.* It is presented within the original time frames to preserve those impressions. Publisher David Lawrence, Jr., of *The Miami Herald* has blessed it with the "full permission and support" of the newspaper, for which I am grateful.

Al Burt

Prelude

The day stays bold and fresh in memory, a sliver of time when family happenings unexpectedly took focus and fit into history. For the first time I saw my parents as Southern refugees, driven by hard times at the old home and drawn by the Florida Boom to the kind of land promised in mail-order catalogs.

For me, then, the family became a personal footnote in the story of how seductive Florida welcomed opportunists and dreamers and escapees of all kinds, and with them built a turbulent megastate. If this new and unsteady giant sputtered along short of its ideals, it was understandable, and it was just one more way I identified with it that day at a family funeral.

An overpoweringly sweetish smell of flowers and the soft sounds that accompany quiet tears reaffirmed the gentle but firm grip of family roots, and the ritual at hand acknowledged how easily those roots can be torn away.

I had gone back to my parents' native place, in those low foothills of northeast Georgia that range up toward the Blue Ridge Mountains, on a journey of duty and love. I went to bury a cousin and a friend. He was my age, and at the time that was sixty. The trip stimulated not only memories but new thoughts about who I was and how I got to be that person.

On one side of a fresh grave streaked with red clay rose the copper-spired Glade Methodist Church (the spire a gift from my Uncle Marvin), and on the other there spread fields of winter-burned grasses where cotton once grew. In between, the shocked remnants of a clannish family gathered, saying good-bye to a man they considered still young. During and after the ceremony, there was much to ponder.

On fields like those, I had learned as a boy on summer vacations to pick cotton, considering it a lark, working beside this departed cousin, his father, and his brother, all of whom welcomed me to their world as an amiable but laughably inept Floridian, which meant foreigner.

Everything about that funeral remains clear: the cold day, the hurt faces, the bleak landscape. Inside one wing of the redbrick church, on a long table covered by vinyl cloth, neighbors and friends put out a huge array of food as an expression of love for a family that had little appetite. For me, not having been back there in a long time, every thing and every person had high dimension and great significance.

As the day stretched on, there was the winter sunset that colored the sky a celebratory orange and royal purple. Mostly, though, there were these gentle people who had been hurt by the death of one who died out of turn, ahead of his father, ahead of his older brother and sister, ahead of so many older aunts and uncles and cousins. The order of things was not right and was, therefore, disturbing.

Their grief created a kind of archaic splendor, the emotions of another age, perhaps another century, one in which there were no things more important than family and church and trying to do the impossible: clinging to them forever.

Thinking about it all, the personal story folded into the long, disinterested look of history—how a tight family wandered from the old home and splintered, against its wishes, each mile and each year and each christening and each funeral widening the gaps and altering the structure. No matter how differently lives evolved, though, most remained marked to some degree by where they originated. There was important knowledge, strength, and identity in that.

₡ The Burts came over from Scotland, although the name is regarded as English. They came into New England, Virginia, and North Carolina. My branch of the family settled in Halifax County, North Carolina. In

1825, after William Burt died, his widow Mary and their three children left North Carolina and moved to an area of northeast Georgia called Enterprise, in the Broad River Valley. In 1879, her son, Emesley Parks Burt, gave land and helped found a Methodist church, still known as Burts Chapel. The family spread out from there.

Exactly 100 years later, in 1925, my parents journeyed away from the bitterly cold and hard winters of their parents' rural community, called the Glade, just a few miles from Burts Chapel. They moved away from rich soil but nevertheless difficult farm lives, away from a land where living things tended to put down long taproots and stay put, no matter what, away from the security of a large, caring family, and sallied off to sample the illusory Florida dream propagandized by the Boom.

They left for a come-on spiel of good times for all. They moved to the sandy and mostly infertile flatlands and glamorously attractive waterways of Jacksonville, Florida, where there were supposed to be jobs for all, jobs that did not involve plowing a mule. They came to a land that frequently demanded only shallowly set pancake roots, the kind that can easily be yanked up and reset someplace else. There was a magic about the new place, an unreality. Horizons stretched wider and broader, forever bending the family in newly different directions.

All of it seemed so starkly simple that day of the funeral.

The Burts, somewhat like the Scots and the Irish, or the Spanish or the Italians or the Greeks, had emigrated from an old country. The difference was that their "old country" was Georgia. Their migration stirred the dreams, created the excitements, and brought the traumas that true immigrants nearly always encounter.

Mother and Dad arrived in Florida with a year-old daughter, Frances. Two years later, in 1927, I came along, named Alvin Victor Burt, Jr. The week before my birth, Mother went back home to share the big event with the two sets of grandparents, who lived less than a mile apart at the Glade. I was born in a two-story frame house that had four bedrooms, each with a fireplace, a house dissected by two long halls with high ceilings. It sat on a red hill. A broad porch that extended around two sides of the house overlooked my grandfather's general store. A week after my birth, Mother came back home to Jacksonville. Forever after, I claimed dual citizenship: I was both a native Georgian and a native Floridian. It was arguable. The family bought a two-story white house on the corner of 19th and Hubbard streets in Jacksonville. That was home until I went away seeking my own. In 1937, my brother, Jim, came along and the family decided it was complete.

The house had a low brick wall around it, about two feet above the sidewalk; large oak trees shaded the street perimeter. Dad regularly whitewashed the lower tree trunks, just as they did back in Georgia. Evenings, I would sit on that wall, smelling the aroma of Mother's supper cooking, waiting for the whistle signaling five o'clock, meaning it would soon be time for Dad's old black Model A to come shuddering down the street. That meant it was time to eat.

In those days, Jacksonville had a municipal alarm clock called Big Jim, a 32-inch copper whistle mounted atop the old waterworks down at First and Main streets (later, it was moved to the south side). Big Jim could be heard all over town, blowing 30-second blasts regularly to announce the critical times of day: 7 A.M., at 12 noon to indicate the lunch break, at 1 to remind everyone that it was time to go back to work, and at 5 to mark the end of the workday. If it blew any other time, there probably was a local emergency, though on occasion it might sound off to celebrate a special event. We kept time by Big Jim, a valued part of life in the city.

That time of growing up blurs now. The memories edit themselves, and the freshest ones seem to be those that have significance in retrospect rather than what seemed important then.

Several times during my early teenage years, I spent summers with my grandparents in Georgia, getting acquainted with the "old world" from which my parents came. I also saw what real farm life was like. I tried my hand at milking cows, picking cotton, helping slaughter hogs, sweeping dirt yards with freshly cut dogwood brooms, experiencing a kitchen that produced a banquet for every meal, attending sometimes fire-eating revivals, collecting eggs from the henhouse before breakfast, rabbit hunting with a .22 rifle, skinny-dipping in a woodsy pond known as "the Baptizin' Hole," a name earned because the Baptists once used it to immerse converts.

That taste of the old life flavored the early years. Those summer vacations became a delightful zip back into a previous time. Whatever the countering drawbacks and pluses of isolation and old attitudes, the Glade forever remained a special place to me. I could see why my parents left; I could see how the family and the place drew them back.

❦ My family summers in Georgia ended for the most part in 1946, after the war was over, when I entered the University of Florida and was introduced to another, still larger world. Mostly, I floundered about trying to understand that world and my place in it, the classic search. After graduation, I taught English briefly and then went into journalism, first with United Press in Atlanta, then the *Atlanta Journal*, the *Jacksonville Journal*, and in 1955 *The Miami Herald*, where I first served as a sportswriter and then in a series of posts that included being city editor, Latin America editor, and finally roving Florida columnist.

While I was Latin America editor, covering a civil war in the Dominican Republic the morning of May 6, 1965, my friend and photographer Doug Kennedy and I made news of our own. During a cease-fire that was enforced by U.S. Marines and paratroopers, Doug and I were shot as we approached a Marine barricade. We followed all the rules, had all the necessary permissions (including a personal assurance from U.S. Ambassador Tapley Bennett and U.S. Army General Bruce Palmer), but a group of nervous young Marines fired on us against orders. They had been taking sniper fire and they were jumpy, but still there seemed to me no worthy excuse for the incident. A military spokesman called it "tragic." I was hit by .30-caliber machine-gun and small-caliber rifle fire nine times, hospitalizing me for a couple of months and leading in later years to a permanent disability that required me to walk with two canes and to buy a wheelchair. Doug, hurt worse, spent a year in Walter Reed Hospital and later died from causes that might have been related to the shooting, though that could not be proved medically.

In 1973, when my exceptional friend Larry Jinks, the executive editor, proposed that I become a roving Florida columnist, my life somehow took on the aspect of ordained order and structure. It was as though everything before, from my parents' migration all the way to my injuries in the Dominican Republic, had been schooling for this.

All my life, except for a couple of working years away, I had lived in Florida. My plan now was to study it as I would a foreign country, to try to see it with new eyes, to do my best to understand it. For the next two decades and more, with my wife, Gloria, as full partner, advisor, and bon vivant companion, we traveled to new places and clocked changes to familiar places, watching the future Florida taking shape.

I now look back on the two decades that followed as probably the most turbulent in modern Florida history. The massive population shifts so quickly applied overwhelming stresses that the state had not time, knowledge, or resources for adequate responses.

I tried to write about the things that I thought were important, even though they might not have been the stuff of headlines. I looked for human situations and conflicts and dilemmas that indicated how things were going for the mass of Floridians in their daily lives. I looked for things that influenced lives in subtle ways—those that didn't always leave big tracks and didn't always make big noises and didn't always attract big crowds, the things in daily life that indicated values and lifestyle.

This was journalism of a sort, not science. I utilized impressions and intuitions, not just police reports or council minutes, not just facts and statistics. My stuff rarely came out of the courthouse but often out of a neighborhood house. I looked for the things that foreshadowed the new character and the new dimensions taking shape in Florida. I tried to explain some of the shock and disorientation that came with rapid changes, and how old customs and traditions and natural beauty were being exchanged for new conveniences and new opportunities and greater diversity. Over the years with building melancholy I reached the horseback conclusion that Florida, a great state, was putting itself in jeopardy.

It was fun, despite that. Things change. As an oldtimer in Melrose lamented to me once, "Nothing is like it used to be, not even the roads. They used to go somewhere, to somebody's house or to somebody's store. Now they just keep on going, on and on, to no place special." He saw it as a structure encouraging a kind of land-bound version of the Flying Dutchman, the legend of sailors doomed never to reach a port. It distressed him.

In Florida, though, the whole thing is special, so you can take any road. As you will see here, Gloria and I did, and we enjoyed every minute and mile of it.

The View from Headquarters

The mythic dimensions of long, crookedly beautiful Florida line up off center and produce offkey harvests. The effect can be jarring to dreamers looking for sweetness and symmetry in paradise. Reality puts a bitter-sweet bite into the flavors and tilts the lines and the appetites toward the odd, making an enduring love for Florida—after the vacation glow wears off—an acquired taste, like mullet or avocados.

Even the two capitols, which offer the most inspiring man-made view in the state, sit way up North virtually in the shadow of Georgia, far from the population centers down South. As you approach the Capitol Center on Tallahassee's Apalachee Parkway, you go down a little hill and then you start back up another, and then before you rises a scene that symbolizes the wonderful peculiarities of Florida: two capitols, in all their contrasting magnificence, high on a hill and gleaming under the sun, Cracker headquarters in heaven.

The graceful old capitol (originally completed in 1845, the restored version opened in 1982), with its peppermint awnings and graceful dome sprouting a tiny flagpole, showers you with a full sense of state history. A few wise old fogeys, renegade history buffs among the patriotic lovers of malls and interstates, narrowly saved it from being torn down when the new one came along.

The modern 22-story capitol (1978) looks over its shoulder, Big Brother's temple of Oz with two squared-off legislative hall shoulders, blocky and precise enough to have been sired by a computer, ready not only to sort out the future in square bytes but to start eating them as well.

Inside, grandeur mixes with the mysteries of politics. The trappings encourage the temptation to believe that some kind of magic exists here. Gardeners ride lifts to polish the leaves in multifloored shafts of greenery. Legislators posturing world-weariness rise from rosewood desks in amphitheaters and speak while others thrust thumbs into the air, pointing up or down, to indicate reaction. An electronic scoreboard records it all, lending an air of sport to the business of lawmaking.

Here to these great temples, Florida turns to find order for lives reeling from change. Inflation, crime, growth, environment become fears to be assuaged. Sebring might plead for legislative leverage in getting a traffic signal. Cedar Key might ask for a new boat ramp. Sanibel might seek new ideas for avoiding population glut. The petitions can be endless and varied: Miami wants help with refugee problems, a legislator proposes the gallstone as the official state gem, migrant farm workers pray for more protective laws. Things high and low, urgent and convenient, occasionally frivolous, compete for attention.

The two capitols make up the center of Tallahassee and the center of the state, once you accept the idea of the center being off center. It is no problem for me. I have gotten used to it.

In 1824, three years after the United States acquired Florida as a territory, Tallahassee became the capital because it was convenient middle ground between Florida's two most important cities, Pensacola and St. Augustine. The hold of history somehow kept it there.

The city strikes me as Florida's most formal. Traditionally less distracted by keeping up than with keeping on, it has tried to hold on to its old manners and customs while puffing along in the rat race with the rest of us. Tallahassee's hills and trees, the awareness of history (street names: Adams, Monroe, Madison, Duval, Lafayette, Calhoun), and the importance it accords an aura of charm deliver an elegant blend.

About it, to most visitors at least, there is a feeling of solidity and stability and respectability, despite the annual brawls of the legislature. It would not surprise me to discover that, per capita in Tallahassee, more people wear coats and ties and practice the civilizing constraints of public courtesy than anywhere else in the state. However, neither would it surprise me to learn that the percentage has dwindled there as it has elsewhere.

Tallahassee speech patterns and life routines still seem to have an overlay of Southern grace. They encourage the hopeful speculation that even those newcomers who have come here to conquer will find, after a few years, that what happens has not been conquest but seduction. No one suggests that the mass of people, and especially not the higher-echelon politicians and state employees, necessarily slur their words with biscuits-and-grits accents or shuffle about in slow motion and practice the maddening indirections of Southern legend. Actually, most seem to stay in a trot and to make conscious efforts to enunciate precisely and to make points with sometimes dismaying bluntness, if not Yankee efficiency. This frequently produces a speech pattern that emerges marvelously Southern-sensitive but with some syllables jacked up in the middle as though to correct a sagging roof and others neatly clipped on the end as though to spruce up the back porch. I personally can relate to that because I have been trying to do it for years, you-all.

Straightening out those tumbled-down old words without taking away the Southern distinction seems also to suggest a preferred Tallahassee style in many things: polite compromise without submission, a little repair and reform in government without radical change, needed or not. In a city where the massive presence of government makes politics the life machinery, it seems natural and proper for this kind of human lubrication to be preserved.

One reason could be that the grove of large state buildings, titled to show that they have assumed responsibility for almost every sort of problem Florida has or expects to develop, creates an ambience not only of tradition but power as well.

"Tallahassee is more a matter of attitude than buildings and facilities," Malcolm Johnson, an old friend, sometimes cranky conservative and longtime editor of *The Tallahassee Democrat*, once corrected me. From 1974 on, he did this periodically. "Even newcomers usually catch on pretty quick to the notion of a way of life that involves grace and courtesy and hospitality. Combine that with people who love trees and plants, and pay homage to history, and it explains why you have a special place," he said.

In his time "Tubby" Johnson (as he was called back in Jacksonville when he was growing up and while working two years for the *Jacksonville Journal*) knew Tallahassee and state politics as well as anyone. In 1937, at age twenty-four, he caught a Seaboard "motorcoach" (a train consisting of a diesel engine and one passenger car) out of Jacksonville and arrived three hours later during a legislative session. As he once described it in a column, he "dropped his bags at the top of the Democrat steps just before noon deadline and was promptly put to work writing headlines."

Johnson began Tallahassee newspapering in a yeasty time, when the rough edges and loose ends of the legislature, joined to the hazards of a full-blown depression, created a frontier rawness. One wing of the old capitol had not yet been finished and the other had not yet been planned. He quickly caught what he called the Tallahassee "contagion," cheerleading and crusading for his vision of an elegant Tallahassee, and never wanted to work anywhere else. His time included 14 years as an Associated Press correspondent (11 as bureau chief) before he returned to the *Democrat* in 1954, staying until retirement in 1978.

He told wondrous tales of political mischief and misdeeds, sometimes leading to public violence. A favorite related how Steve Trumbull (*The Miami Herald* writer in the 1950s) had been briefly barred from the press gallery following a dispute over some casually critical remarks about a state senator. These remarks were relayed to the fellow in question, and, as Johnson wrote in the *Democrat,* Steve then "ran his chin into [state] Senator Sandy MacArthur's fist." Briefly, the entire press corps boycotted the press gallery in Trumbull's support.

Johnson's more serious political commentaries placed controversies into the perspective of history. He persisted and often prevailed in efforts to perpetuate his Tallahassee vision with campaigns to save the city's trees, to rescue native flora being uprooted by expressways and to replant it along rights of way (the Upsy-Daisy Plant Society), and to fund time in summer camps (Funders, Inc.) for needy boys and girls.

Allen Morris, a former newsman, longtime clerk of the Florida house of representatives, and the creator of the essential *Florida Handbook,* also remembered the days—before the new capitol—when the political scene was "a temporary work camp," where families and friends and reporters milled in the chambers with the lawmakers. He came to Tallahassee as a reporter for the Associated Press in 1934 and attended his first legislative session in 1941. No one knew more stories about legislators, or told them better, than Allen Morris. He recited a series of them to me in 1979 and generously furnished copies of his speeches and other work.

"It was a noisy chamber," he said of his early legislative experience. "There was the clatter of kicked spittoons and collapsing metal folding chairs, the hum of a hundred conversations, the shout of members trying to make themselves heard without microphones. The Speaker could isolate a Member by seating him on the back row (where he had difficulty being heard). . . . The open galleries contributed to the bedlam and to the haze of tobacco smoke which hung over the Chamber."

Morris said members milled about in the chamber with the secretaries, families, and the press. So casual was the scene that Morris remembered sitting among the three members of the Dade delegation and, when a member had to be away from his desk, pushing the switch of the voting machine when the absent member signaled him to do so. Secretaries took dictation on the floor during sessions because most members didn't have private offices. The size of the spittoons, said Morris, differed from the senate to the house—the house used low, nickel-plated spittoons, and the senate had high brass ones.

Members shouted hoarsely over the din for the speaker of the house to recognize them. During the time of Governor David Sholtz (1933–37), a fire escape ran the short half-story from the window in his office to the ground outside. During the Depression, the governor used it to escape job seekers. "His dash out the window often was to a men's room in the basement," Morris said. The governor, without a rest room of his own, had to share a public facility. Job seekers followed him even there. Morris conjured up a picture of him being forced to sit glumly while they pleaded for favors.

Morris remembered his dilemmas as a reporter out of Miami, fresh to Tallahassee, when an enraged representative from Dixie County stood up and shouted, "Chicken-ree . . . chicken-ree." He was puzzled until an oldtimer advised him about the language problem. The word was *chicanery*.

In those days, too, delegates sometimes spoke too quickly. Morris said one senator publicly charged a legislative messenger with commenting that senators were a bunch of "crooks and thieves." The messenger defended himself: "Oh, no, I didn't say that. I don't know how it got out on you." Another young representative, speaking about money matters during the 1970s, described himself on the floor as a "physical conservative" and complained about a proposed bill that would take "food out of the pockets" of his constituents.

Morris remembered another house member who had trouble with the language. He passed a bill intending to give his county commissioners a $100 a month raise, but the bill said the raise would be given "per annum payable in 12 equal monthly installments." The raise would be $8.33 a month, not $100.

Until 1968, the state constitution required a bill to be read in full at the time of final consideration (a requirement frequently ignored). During the 1939 session, Morris said, members used that requirement as a delaying tactic by requiring a 300-page school code be read ahead of a bill they were trying to defeat. As a countertactic, one member read parts of the bill in French, another man in Portugese, another in Yiddish. The filibusterers protested they could not tell whether the entire bill was being read. Members shouted at one another. There was pandemonium, Finally, one man shouted, "Mr. Speaker, this is the goddamndest thing I ever heard of."

Morris quoted the lead paragraph of an Associated Press story describing the scene: "Five languages, including the profane, were used in a filibuster in the Florida House of Representatives tonight." Equally memorable was a three-day filibuster conducted by John E. Mathews, Sr., of Jacksonville. As it dragged on, an uncomfortable Mathews asked the Speaker to clear the galleries of women and children while he relieved himself in a spittoon. He got a recess instead.

A benchmark of progress came in 1965, when house speaker E. C. Rowell announced that henceforth all legislative secretaries would be required to take a typing test. Until then, applicants' files carried such administrative appraisals as "good legs" or "living doll."

In those good old days, according to Morris, the end of a 60-day session could be a sentimental time: "There were those who privately said, 'I love you honey, but the session's over'."

Beyond the grace and elegance of Tallahassee that Johnson so loved, and the legislative highs and lows that fascinated Morris, there is another, contrasting image: that of Tallahassee, sitting up there loftily in North

Florida, away from the centers of population, away from the places where life boils and whistles more conventionally and erratically, viewing Florida as from a comfortable skybox. Envious ordinary citizens might wonder whether the wonderful civility and privileged atmosphere, the Asian teak and African ebony legislative chambers, the long marble halls, the easy-chair legislative seats, all that heady power and atrium-tranquilizing unreality might dull true empathy for skint-knuckle or street-bruised lives out there beyond the gavels and PA systems, on the streets and in the trenches. That image creates concerns about whether such a fine legislative refuge links as persuasively as it might to citizen anxiety about zoning and education and crime, about the upsetting backwinds of growth and development, about the fear and curdling of will that can occur where the houses are less imposing, the accents more mixed, and where the state armies run thin.

From the observation deck atop the 22-story capitol, you can see Florida in all directions, all the way to the horizon. It is a gorgeous view from headquarters. You can see the government buildings and Tallahassee, and beyond that you can see trees and gentle hills, a lake or two, and finally long stretches of greenery that fade into the horizon. Windows cover all sides. You can hear the wind whistle faintly up there, but you are not cold; the rain falls, and you do not get wet; the traffic honks below, and you do not have to jump or dodge. You can imagine the slow, studied percolation of history all about you.

From Tallahassee, the throne room, the kingdom rolls out—all the way south, 600 miles to the Keys, and all the way west, 200 miles to Pensacola, and all the way east, another 200 miles or so, to Fernandina Beach—with extraordinary diversity. Out there is the fabled La Florida, exotic enough for the careless to call it paradise, beautiful enough for almost all to love, but too complex and changeable for easy understanding.

❦ No better pioneer example of Snowbird trials have I heard than the one given me by Mrs. J. D. McCarthy in Okeechobee, who told me her family story in 1975, a tape-recorded conversation for purposes of local history. By her count, it took her 16 years to decide she loved the Florida peculiarities. In 1913 her father, a Nebraskan, read about land for sale in Florida, about dreams for sale at $5 an acre. He bought but later went back to Nebraska and turned the property over to a son, who opened a grocery and feed store in Okeechobee, not far from the largest lake wholly within the confines of the mainland United States. In 1917, the U.S. Army drafted him for duty in World War I.

Another brother, Mrs. McCarthy's husband, came down to run the store in his place. In Nebraska, her husband had been a teamster. When they came to Florida they had been married for two years.

The McCarthys took a train out of Omaha one Sunday morning, reached Chicago later that day, and then a problem developed. Trying to buy tickets to continue the trip, they discovered the clerks never had heard of Okeechobee and couldn't even find it on the map. The McCarthys settled for tickets to Jacksonville, but even there Okeechobee was regarded as a frontier city. They reached New Smyrna Beach by 2 P.M. Thursday, and the train pulled in to Okeechobee at 11 that night, a five-day trip.

She woke up to a new world. Ranchers drove cattle down the middle of the streets. Some of the animals wandered about freely. There was no fence law. Rowdy catfishermen off the big lake and cowboys from the nearby ranches spent Saturday nights drinking moonshine and roughhousing. Sunday mornings, a few enterprising townspeople would scratch around in the dirt streets to find money that the combatants had lost. Seminole Indians milled around the store, one of them named Billy Bowlegs. "He was a big gray-haired man, very nice, very friendly," Mrs. McCarthy said. He would go into her kitchen and eat lunch sometimes. "J. D. would get a plate and a knife and fork, and he [Bowlegs] would pick it up with his fingers," she said. J. D. bought snake, alligator, and other wild animal hides from the Indians for resale.

The McCarthys drove a Model T 30 miles to Fort Pierce to attend the nearest Catholic church, the car threatening to shake apart on the bumpy roads when it got up to 25 miles per hour. Families and customers lived out in the the woods. "When we delivered groceries, we would laugh and say that our wagon could knock bugs off the trees on both sides of those narrow roads at the same time," she said.

She saw the Okeechobee courthouse built in 1923, lived through the 1928 hurricane, when roofs blew off some buildings and the winds drove the lake water into the edges of town. Next morning, they found people hanging in the trees. President Herbert Hoover came to inspect the damage and afterward had the Hoover Dike built around the lake to contain the water. After that, people began to talk about Okeechobee becoming "the Chicago of the South." It did become "The Speckled Perch Capital of the World." The lake was full of perch, the fish commonly called crappie, but Okeechobeeans tastefully avoided calling their town the Crappie Capital of the World.

The Depression came along, and two local banks failed. "Everybody was saying everything was all right, and all of a sudden the banks just failed." The McCarthys, in her words, "burned up $25,000 or $35,000 worth" of debts on paper. "Some people came back 30 years later and paid us," she said. "Others just forgot it." There were enough gardens on the farms, catfish in the lake, and cattle on the ranches to keep people from starving, but there was little money.

"I was homesick for about 16 years," Mrs. McCarthy said. In 1919, when her brother came home from the war, she and J. D. drove back to Nebraska in a Model T, planning to stay, but they didn't. J. D. couldn't take the winters anymore; they bothered his rheumatism. The McCarthys returned to the grocery and feed store, but warm winters still didn't keep her from being homesick. Her brother went into the plumbing business.

Okeechobee, to a Nebraskan, seemed like a foreign country. "I never heard of grits until I came down here, or black-eyed peas. We always had English peas at home. But I like black-eyed peas now. Okra, I never ate that at home, but I like it now," she said.

One day a man came into the store, sat around talking for a while. "Well," Mrs. McCarthy remembered him saying, "I guess I'd better go and carry my mule down to the crick." "Why don't you ride him?" she asked, surprised. That drew a laugh.

At Christmas, there was no snow. Most of the year, heat and humidity were fierce. Every day, mosquitoes and cockroaches and an immense variety of other bugs buzzed and crawled around. Possums, raccoons, otters, skunks, alligators, and snakes shared the land, sometimes even the town. "One of the men in town had a little pet fawn, the cutest little thing, and it'd come to the backdoor and I'd feed it apples and things," she said.

The McCarthys lived in the back of the store. She had many sleepless nights, for a variety of reasons, including a couple of donkeys that slept under a store canopy. "They would stomp all night long, to get the mosquitoes off, you know. You couldn't drive them away," she said.

A man rode in on horseback one evening, saying he was snakebit. "It killed him," Mrs. McCarthy said. "Somebody brought the snake hide to

J. D. and wanted him to buy it. So J. D. bought it and had it tanned. Afterward we heard they were building a new hotel in West Palm Beach and this man that was killed belonged to a club that was building it." Some of the members came over to Okeechobee and wanted to buy that snakeskin from J. D. "They were going to raffle it off and give the money to the widow," Mrs. McCarthy said. "J. D. just gave it to them, and they raffled it off and got $25 or $35 for her."

Finally, Mrs. McCarthy looked back on it all with pleasure. The perspective of the years turned hardships into Florida adventures. It took a lot of time, but Mrs. McCarthy acquired the taste.

The job for me, as I set out in September of 1973 to take a fresh look at the state where I had lived nearly all my life, amounted to a voyage for the discovery of the familiar, to find out about home; not only to write about Florida as I saw it but to know the Florida that others had discovered and to share that, too. It surprised me to learn that it would not be as easy as I thought.

As it did for Mrs. McCarthy in Okeechobee, for me the range of geography and weather that the entire state offered, the immense differences in all forms of life, the foreign influences from Nebraska or New Jersey or from the Caribbean and Central America, added to the puzzle and the pleasure.

Florida starts in the subtropics and slowly rises into the true temperate zone, the geography and all living things taking on different looks as the elevation goes from sea level to hilly, the terrain from desertlike to swampy, the soil from sugar sands and rich muck to red clay. The blossoms change from orchids and frangipani to azaleas and dogwoods, the people from international sophistication to Cracker commonality, the accents from the bobtailed syllables of New York and from the distinctive, fast-breaking Spanish of the Cubans to the mysteries of Haitian Creole and Southern mushmouth (like mine). Gourmet delicacies switch from stone crabs and mango to mullet and grits.

All that would be formidable enough to know well. Near impossibility develops when you add massive in-migration (the Florida population jumped from 528,000 in 1900 to 2,771,305 in 1950 to some 14 million in 1996). Add to that the seasonal migrations of tourists (about 40 million annually in recent years), a million or more residents annually moving from one place to another within Florida, agricultural workers migrating seasonally, a steady stream of Floridians moving out (an estimated one moving out for each two coming in), and a stunning picture of transience emerges.

Almost everything in Florida moves, like the ocean tides and the seasons, in patterns or cycles, not always rhythmic ones. From one year to the next, the familiar might surprise you; from one decade to the next, it almost certainly will.

One winter season, the story goes, an amused Snowbird encountered an old Cracker in crowded South Florida. "Lots of weird people down here," the Snowbird said patronizingly. "Yeah," the Cracker replied, looking him over carefully, "But they ain't near so many in August as they is this time of year."

There are so many Floridas. In his 1875 guidebook, *Florida: Its Scenery, Climate, and History*, the poet Sidney Lanier offered this definition: "The question of Florida is a question of an indefinite enlargement of many people's pleasures and of many people's existences as against the killing ague of modern life. . . . Here one has an instinct to repose broad-faced upward, like fields in the fall, and to lie fallow under suns and airs."

The state's mythic dimensions and bittersweet flavors lead an explorer in many directions. From Cracker headquarters, in Tallahassee, it looks simple. Knee-deep in the swamp or the sand, with the chiggers and the no-see-ums biting you, or stuck in traffic on what should be a free-flowing interstate, it gets more interesting.

A Sense of Florida

In the sweetly ragged patch of scrub country that I call home, life takes on a comfortably defensive droop. Few but the patient and deliberate live here happily, for appreciation of its sterling but prickly character requires time and persistence. With those qualities, though, come understanding and true love, the kind a Cracker mama feels for a loved child likely to be called ugly by strangers.

Maybe the scrub does not primp and shine quite like Naples or Vero Beach, but we who live here do not mind. Maybe it does not have the grandeur of the Keys or the mystery of the Everglades or the come-lately glamour of Destin and Amelia Island, but by a different measuring stick we find it beautiful.

The scrub, ancient and harsh terrain, yet in many ways delicate, occurs in several areas of the state. When the oceans fell millions of years ago, it probably was the first part of Florida to rise out of the water. As sea levels dropped, beach dunes in effect wandered inland, and on those infertile hills and flats the thriftiest of plants and animals made precarious life. Remnants of it occur near Ocala, down the central ridge and along some coastal areas. Where they can, developers shower the old dunes (attractively high ground) with water and fertilizer and green them over with things more attractive to newcomers. What is more valuable to Florida, after all, another dollar or an old dune?

My little patch of scrub (alt. 180 feet), a wooded six acres by a clear lake about 25 miles east of Gainesville, occurs in an area where there are no true cities but many contending capitals, all small and individual and feisty. My capital is Melrose, an 1890s winter resort served by steamboats on the lakes, until railroads, paved roads, and airplanes made more conventionally pleasing places accessible to the Snowbirds. Nearby there are Keystone Heights and Hawthorne and Interlachen and Orange Heights, among others, all with quietly interesting histories to tell if you will just sit down on somebody's porch and listen.

The scrub landscape, to me, looks like backsliding desert. Scraggly growth, anchored by stunted trees, palmettos and rosemary bushes and other scratchy things, all of them finding nourishment where none appears to exist, make it seem inhospitable. Beautiful oases come in clusters and streaks. On deeply greened land islands, giant live oaks and toweringly tall canopies of pines give dimension to the horizon. In high contrast, hundreds of lakes (some lined by cypresses) socket into those bone-dry hills and create a shade of holiday Florida, offering swimming and fishing and boating and scenic vistas. Dominating earth colors are broken and ornamented here and there by dogwoods and azaleas and dazzling arrays of seasonal wildflowers. Few tourists get up enough courage to wander away from the interstates and into these scrubby backwoods, and even fewer understand or appreciate what they see when they do. Bless them.

This is a piece of old Florida, where the Snowbirds have seeped in but have not taken over, at least not yet. Natives get respect here, if not honor. History and heritage remain prized by many. The biggest buildings are schools and churches. Houses scatter through the woods and around the lakes. People meet communally at the post office or library or the grocery store or at preaching on Sunday. By urban Florida standards, the population is thin. For years the area provided weekend and vacation homes for city folk from Jacksonville and Gainesville. Following a Florida pattern, it evolved from that into a commuters' retreat and then turned into retirement country for those who seek a quieter Florida, away from the crowds, away from the concrete and asphalt heat islands along the coast. Melrose distances itself from what the late Florida entertainer Gamble Rogers called "that honky-tonk for children, Disney World," by enough miles to make it a two-to-three-hour drive, which is almost enough.

Creatures as exotic as the gopher tortoise and coral snake, and as common as the raccoon and the rattlesnake, do well in the scrub. Exotics, like the transplanted South Floridian and the coyote and the loquat, thrive if given the smallest chance. Armadillos root up fragile lawns. Deer roam into many yards, including mine, eating the spring leaves off plantings, nibbling at the wild cherries, sharing cracked corn with armies of squirrels. Bobcats and foxes leave tracks. Bream, black bass, and catfish inhabit the lakes, along with alligators and turtles and occasional otters.

This piece of scrub lies approximately halfway between the Gulf and Atlantic coasts, and so has access to each. The Santa Fe, the fabled Suwannee, the Ichetucknee (famed as a tubers' paradise), and the northward-flowing St. Johns rivers are short drives away. Clear, bubbling springs, like the one that fuels the Ichetucknee, enliven forests to the northwest and southwest.

Unlike South Florida, the scrub country schedules all seasons. When the chuck-will's-widow mounts a stump and begins to whistle at night and the lightning bugs begin blinking in the woods, we know it is spring, a distinct time. When the rains slow and the dogwoods turn yellow and red, competing with the maples for brilliance, and later the migrating sandhill cranes begin to return, the air thins out cool and dry and we know it is fall. Snowbirds on the interstates tell us it is winter, which brandishes a few freezes but usually gives way after three or four days to enchantingly mild weather enhanced by local headlines gloating about the ice and snow up north. Like the rest of Florida, we have long and hot and usually wet summers. The rain leaches quickly through the scrub sands and refreshes the lakes. Hurricanes rarely reach this far inland, though it is possible, and we worry about them. Everyone needs a bogeyman or two.

Once you have developed a taste for the peculiarities of the scrub country, no other place seems quite tangy enough. On most days life takes on the easy pace of a Sunday morning. At its best, some say that in this quiet there is a hint of what awaits the repentant man. Crime and politics and taxes find natively creative ways to intrude, as they do everywhere, but the scrub country tends to downsize them. Most of the time, they have to invade in low gear.

Deep sand and owlish old-timers and two-rut roads, sandspurs and fierce lightning, general stores and neighbors in the old style who watch and help, the lack of cable televison (satellite dishes flourish)—all these bless and deprive and demand at once, establishing wonderfully human perspectives.

A beautiful egret, the symbol of the Audubon Society, sauntered up from the lake one day like a friendly messenger from the wild come to our yard, and we were proud there was a visitor there to see it. The elegance of the bird—its long, black legs, the gracefully toe-dripping stride, the snow-white feathering—encouraged reverence in us, but the feeling was not necessarily universal.

"Them pond birds," said the old-timer sitting on my front porch, pointing to the egret, "is good eatin'. They'll fry up like a chicken."

Like that, the scrub country charms and jars you at the same time. A variety of such reminders notify you that old times and old attitudes can hang on—despite air-conditioning and running water and public libraries and the beneficiary waves of enlightenment that radiate from the nearby University of Florida campus—and still require confronting. The reminders take the pain out of nostalgia.

The scrub is a place apart, to be sure, but that doesn't matter to those of us who call it home. For me, this is soul Florida. All of Florida is home, but this is the heart of it. Knowing these things about it, living here since 1974, and before that growing up an hour and a half away (in Jacksonville) and spending many youthful summers and holidays in the Melrose area, make it familiar and comfortable, like blood-and-bone kin.

The many years, and the many trials and flourishes, of living—the seasoning of births and deaths among cherished ones, migrations that brought new friends and sometimes took away old ones, the rituals of weddings and funerals, the testing by illnesses and divorces and disagreements—tempered and strengthened the attachment. Identification and commitment provide a special sense of this place. It takes time, Snowbirds.

After living in Miami, after working in Jacksonville and Atlanta and for a brief while in Washington, D.C., after much time traveling in Latin America, this rural home came to me like an earned reward. It prejudiced me newly in favor of open space and greenery. It refreshed and deepened my appreciation of civility and manners and community. Small towns in

Florida have become like the small, distinctive neighborhoods of the city, for which sociologists and architects and planners so often pine. They offer a kind of life that used to be so attractive in the cities but is hard to find there anymore.

During my travels for *The Miami Herald,* a perception grew that Florida's natural treasures and history add distinctive character to its oddly graceful geography and climate, and that these are essential in making it a good place to live and an enduring place to do business. Without those, we might as well be a franchised greenhouse, transferrable to wherever technology creates another greenhouse. Disrespect for the nature of Florida, the cannibalizing of it for short-term profit or pleasure that limits its future, pained me.

My first sortie into the state as Florida columnist—beginning a personal mission and full-time job of rediscovering my home state—began in September, 1973. At the first stop, Sanibel Island, I talked to a gentleman known as "Uncle" Clarence Rutland, a Sanibel pioneer. Executive editor Larry Jinks gave me a proper launching. With a picture of a shirtless Uncle Clarence in his rocking chair, the editors stripped that first story across page one with the headlines: "He Prefers Mosquitoes to Sanibel's Progress" and, inside, "Building the Bridge Was a Mistake, Islander Says." The story seemed quaint at the time, an amusing oldtimer speaking out, but it was a beginning that had legs.

Rutland, born on the west side of Lake Apopka (north of Orlando) in 1890, went to Sanibel Island in 1895, long before there was a bridge, when there still were mosquitoes so thick you could catch them in a bucket, when deer roamed the island, when oysters and clams were plentiful (and safe), and the fishing was easy. Then, as Uncle Clarence saw it, the bridge was built (1963), spray planes killed off the mosquitoes, and people began to swarm in. Everybody on Sanibel made money and that was nice, he said, but the deer disappeared, and the oysters and clams became inedible, and the island atmopshere faded. He wondered whether it might be a shortsighted swap.

From Sanibel, we slowly journeyed up the Gulf Coast and across the Panhandle to Pensacola, gathering folksy stories and columns all the while—a deputy sheriff in Pasco County who celebrated his felony arrests by pasting gold stars on his squad car, natives lamenting the obliteration of history in remote Pine Level, a Cedar Key mayor and hardware store entrepeneur who grew poetic talking about a tub of freshly caught pompano while I sat on a keg of nails and listened to him giving audience to grumbling constituents—and then made our way back by a different route. It took most of a month, setting a pattern and a pace that we followed for years after, searching all of Florida, rambling and absorbing the feel and smell and taste of it, reveling in the adventure.

Out of different mouths, explaining different situations, a recurring note sounded among the Floridians I met: Florida, especially along its coasts, was coming under siege from migrating population growth that it was not prepared to handle, and this re-created again and again the dilemma of the shortsighted swap posed by Uncle Clarence.

"Chickens are unbelievably dumb," I wrote in *The Herald*. "They climb all over each other when eating or drinking. If scared, they pile up and smother, trying to escape. They just don't know enough to scatter out and make room. Cracker wisdom up here in the Panhandle . . . suggests people and chickens are a whole lot alike. Floridians pile up along the coasts. Space enough to live, and water enough to drink, grow short. Still, they pile in."

Before long, traveling and trying to respond to that theme of dilemma, I began to hear people referring to me as an environmentalist, a bad word to some. It surprised me, but I did not care. If so, I was an accidental one, created when run over by the Florida stampede. I had no agenda but discovery. Florida was teaching me its own lessons.

The next 22 years, while I was traveling the state, concerns about the environment went from the fringe to the heart, and I followed them. In the 1970s, environmentalists were thought to be elitists, advocates of esoteric, radical, and perhaps lunatic ideas. That changed.

Today, not every Floridian calls himself an environmentalist or a conservationist—pick your term—but for most Floridians these concerns have become matters of self-defense, not elitist philosophy. When citizens begin to worry about their drinking water, the air they breathe, elbow room at the beach and in the malls, and driving room on the streets, environmentalism becomes personal and compelling, whatever you call it.

In 1970, Florida had a population of 6.7 million; in 1996, about 14 million. Forecasts suggest as many as 32 million by the year 2010. In my two decades-plus on the road, the population of Florida approximately doubled. According to University of Florida's population experts, about half as many Floridians were leaving as arriving. This formula meant approximately 14 million new Floridians arrived in those two decades, and about 7 million Floridians moved out. That turbulent population exchange created extraordinary human static. In the statistics of stress— divorce, suicide, crime, auto accidents—Florida moved up among the national leaders.

A rambling Florida columnist could not help noticing among the delights a chord of unease. A kind of full-moon wackiness invaded the headlines and police reports. In the Florida chapel, calliopes sounded.

Florida was growing up, aging awkwardly, making painful swaps but shedding ignorance and prejudice, gaining new urban status and political clout, achieving new convenience and diversity and enlightened visions. Floridians cheered those gains but not the losses. Was it necessary to disown heritage to make progress? Did we have to turn our state into a facade of some other place, to mimic the manners and customs of some other region, to bring in electricity and running water? The numbers came too fast. There was too little experience dealing with them. The wonders of growth amounted to economic patriotism and swept most complaints away. The economy built on a bet that numbers would solve each new problem all by itself and that the numbers never would stop coming. Adapting creatively and positively to steamrolling change became a catch-up game, and in those years Florida never seemed to catch up.

Once in Florida (especially South Florida) winter was the rush hour. It started after Thanksgiving and continued until April. That changed. The rush hour began to last all year, a sort of circular stampede funneled along the interstates, people coming and going at a trot all the time. The slow off-season all but disappeared.

Even so, the true Snowbird Season—the winter—remains the peak, and with reason. In winter, a kind of magical unreality flourishes in Florida. Visitors look back north toward home with glee, to the snow and the ice and toward urban conditions that make Florida's problems seem small. Fantasy rules. Adventure beckons. There is a sense of being homesteaders in a foreign setting. The population entertains every conceivable human claim but none dominates. There is no orthodoxy, all is motion and change, many little worlds spinning in their own orbits, convened in a place hanging close to the sun.

Visitors feel part of a place apart. They become pleasure pilgrims with curiously fractured identities, not here to sink roots and establish but to frolic. Snow-peppered citizens from Ohio or New York become chapped-lip expatriates from the cold, sharing a warm interlude with fellow-traveling strangers.

They came for comfort and frivolity, and some were moved to gamble (Florida roulette, old-timers call it) that they could build permanence out of this illusion that has tax benefits. It is an old and familiar pattern. Old-timer Frog Smith of North Fort Myers once told me, speaking impishly and in high humor, of how all the strangers (tourists used to be called "strangers") changed the Florida of his youth, that tourists were like hemorrhoids: the ones that came down and went back were not so bad; the ones who came down and stayed really hurt.

Freezing weather up north triggered the migrating instincts of the Snowbirds. Neither modern heaters nor tight insulation nor cheap fuel oil nor comforts of familiar hearth could hold them. They homed in on the sun like so many robins or sandhill cranes or roseate spoonbills. With magnificent determination, they rushed across borders and ran a gauntlet of tacky souvenir stands so that they could exult in paying outrageous prices for bed and board and maybe buy a rubber alligator or a plastic flamingo.

Even if you have seen the Snowbird flight 10 or even 20 times, the sight always impresses. They come cartoonlike over the horizon, blowing frosty smoke and peeling off sweaters as they hit the Georgia border. They fill up the welcome stops and filter through the fast-food restaurants and service stations and the motels, making a bulge that passes down the peninsula in a way that kindles in the imagination the picture of a long, skinny snake swallowing a fat rabbit.

Most wend their way a thousand miles or more to get here, like secular wise men drawn not by a star but the sun. Some flee to the southern half of Florida, but many drop off along the way in other seductive spots. They spread money, the sincerest tribute, and in return they expect a little fantasy and perhaps the chance to expose their pale skins to the attractive risk of melanoma.

Among their assorted styles, tastes, and colors there are the common threads of cheerful expectation, almost as valuable a commodity as their money. They give Florida an extraordinary shot of vigor. They decorate our state like a Christmas tree, an egg-shaped one hanging here, a star-crossed one there, colorfully shirted ones breaking free from old inhibitions, viewing the world from behind tinted glasses, blinking ones and reflecting ones. Sometimes it seems as though the entire peninsula has been outfitted just for them to light it up.

In gratitude, the official state bells peal, the cash registers ring, and old-time Floridians try to stifle the curses that easily come to voice over the inconveniences the Snowbirds create while bringing us gifts that pay our salaries and enliven our economic possibilities. They make our winter season jolly, these displaced ones who break with tradition and do not wish to be home for the holidays, and in reaction we divide our time between being grateful and being irritated.

When we see that flight of the Snowbirds, we try to remember that it is part of an important process, not only the making of new Floridians but the making of a new Florida, the unfolding of bittersweet progress. Opportunities nearly always include jeopardy.

A sense of this beautifully odd place, Florida, has to be at the foundation of any vision for the state, any true acceptance of it as home. A vision, though, is hard to bring into focus when the bits and pieces of so many dreams create an atmosphere of disorder. Knowing its complexities well ("What is an aquifer, Marge?") is difficult even for natives. For newcomers, distracted by illusions and fantasies, equipped with back-home knowledge and customs and standards that do not fit Florida realities, the difficulties multiply.

With a sense of place, there can follow love and commitment and community—all things rare if not endangered in Florida. Without it, the dream eludes. If you were born here, you learn early to absorb and accept all the balances. If you migrate here, it might take years to understand and to embrace the six-month summer, the humidity, the bugs, the hurricanes, the sinkholes, the deep sand, the flat landscapes, the green Christmases, the droughts and floods. That time lag can hurt us all.

Florida beauty boasts peculiar linings. Overwhelming commercial tackiness butts up to natural scenes so beautiful that they deliver religious overtones. Dune deserts neighbor swamps. Flowers bloom in December and January. Homes open up and virtually bite off a piece of the outdoors. Rains and powerful storms fill the summers, and heat lethargy becomes endemic.

To achieve what the poets call a sense of place, or a sense of Florida, involves deciding where you belong and why. You must understand the rewards and the risks of the environment and feel they are reasonably large enough to accommodate your abilities and hopes without undue jeopardy. A sense of place reassures without confining. The place nurtures you and somehow renourishes your strengths when they have been used up. Without it, the seasons of life lose their beginning cycle. Once lost, for peace of mind it must be re-created.

What has happened to Florida—what has interfered with our sense of place—has been a gilding of something that was already golden, a cosmetizing of the old realities to make them look like an outsider's vision of Florida. We have disguised the old grit and character with gloss and glitz. That kind of process hints at dissatisfaction with what natively was here, not true appreciation. Minority natives feel spiritually exiled in the place where they were born. Everything has been a trade-off, a swap—natural treasures for material ones—but we were trading values as well as physical realities. In hindsight, we might have made a better bargain.

◑ The story goes that once there was a Snowbird who made a return visit to Cedar Key, the isolated Gulf Coast fishing village, after many years away. This time the tide was out, and he had not seen that before. The water level had retreated into the Gulf, and those black mudflats and oyster beds and marine junk were not covered with water. They were lying out in the sun, stinking with what we oldtime Floridians regard as marine perfume.

The Snowbird sniffed and stared, unbelieving. "My God," he said, as the story goes, "what a drought you've had since I was here last."

He had not yet reached an understanding with Florida.

◑ Another Snowbird moved to Florida to stay. She was a determined nature lover. She fed birds. She encouraged raccoons. She had a biscuit and a smile for anything alive. One day she found a little brown casing out in the yard, an egg of some kind. She took it in, nurtured it—and eventually it gave birth, to a healthy cockroach.

Florida is a learning experience.

❦ As I sat on my porch one summer morning out there in the woods where I live, I looked out and saw a rabbit swimming in the lake. Rather than romping around in the briar bushes as respectable rabbits do, he was taking a casual swim.

This was not a thoughtful rabbit. He had no sense of place whatsoever. He had left his natural element. He was in fantasyland and enjoying it, but that did not last. Out there he could not run fast, his best defense. He had no other rabbits for company. He had nothing to eat. Finally, inevitably, he grew uncomfortable.

So he came out—and got the ancient reward for being out of place. Two waiting dogs ate him for lunch.

❦ I grew up with the idea that anytime a "For Sale" sign was spiked into the front lawn of a familiar home, it usually meant bad news. Someone in the neighborhood had died or gone broke or had been transferred. Any of those signaled a time of hurting. There were some happy moves but not many. Most involved disruption.

The moving van would roll up like a brassy thief and haul away a collection of nice people and their possessions—people and things that belonged where they already were. That was life gone awry, and it always hurt. To me then, home included the neighborhood. It needed all its parts, and one was being ripped out. The injury would take time to heal.

Even now, those signs bother me a bit because of their great numbers and for what they suggest. In Florida "For Sale" signs are as common as wildflowers. Floridians change homes, coming and going so routinely that few seem to pay much attention. It happens elsewhere but not with such total churning.

While churning stirs the business pot, it also means that Florida never can finish with the multiple strains of masses of people starting over. Think about that: always the presence of freshly torn roots, always the bemusing challenge of facing new customs and new perspectives, always the task of learning to care about new friends and new landscapes and new neighborhoods, always the difficulty of grasping new political nuances and being able to vote in constructive ways.

I should be numb to those "For Sale" signs by now, for they have become little stickpin notices on the trail to a megafuture, but I am not. "For Sale" signs are a poor substitute for wildflowers. That is a personal notion, of course, just my old neighborhood idea at work. In such numbers, the signs are like a twitch or nervous tic in the public persona. When you have too many of them, too often, you suspect serious disorder.

In 1927, the Florida Federation of Women's Clubs asked Florida schoolchildren to choose their favorite bird. They chose the mockingbird, and the legislature passed an act making it official for the state. It was a perfect choice. Something about the mockingbird fits the state so well.

In 1931, there developed a quarrel about Florida's boasts that the mockingbird was the finest singer among birds. Admirers of the nightingale protested, and a sing-off was set up at Bok Tower in Lake Wales, pitting Florida mockingbirds against imported nightingales.

The mockers won. Not only did they have a lovely repertoire, but during the course of the contest they topped out by perfectly mimicking and matching the nightingales' own songs.

It is hard to beat such talent. The mockingbird can cluck like a chicken, meow like a cat, squeak like a wheel, scream like a hawk, or whistle up a dog with a perfect imitation of its master. It can speak with any accent, inflection, or emphasis—without ever forgetting its own unique sense of self and place. In short, the mockingbird has the perfect Florida voice.

Maybe it sings sometimes like a nightingale, but it still feathers out and builds a nest like a mockingbird. Maybe it meows occasionally like a cat, but it retains the mockingbird instincts. Never does it deceive itself into believing it actually has become a nightingale or a cat. The mockingbird, diminished by unanimity and enlarged by variety, delivers the qualities that embrace most gracefully the quarreling counterthemes of Florida.

The mockingbird symbolizes the hopeful but committed Florida citizen—one cautiously adaptive but also one who never abandons its own identity. Its simple gray and white feathering takes on the conservative elegance of a fine business suit alongside the exotic coloring of the migrating birds. The extraordinary talent for mimicry gives it a chameleonic dimension that equips it to sing harmony with whatever shows up, without giving up an individual voice. To have a sense of Florida, the mockingbird has a perfect character.

❧ When I start comparing things now with what they were like 20 or even 50 years ago—as far back as memory is reasonably reliable—the changes are striking. In one lifetime, I have picnicked in fields that became subdivisions and parking lots and even airports, climbed sandy dunes where condos now rise, swum in rivers that became the equivalent of sewers, planted gardens where interstates now race, tumbled down bluffs that gave way to shopping malls.

I saw Florida when it was young, in the 1930s and 1940s (less than 100 years old as a state), and then, as a more professional observer, saw the accelerated aging process take over in the 1970s and 1980s. The beautiful Indian River lagoon, once teeming with fish and bordered with wildlife, struggled against pollution. New cities such as Destin mushroomed. Scientists checked the pulse of the Everglades and clucked that it was dying. Wading birds diminished. Wetlands withered. Even mullet, once a baitfish, became scarce. We feared for the survival of wildlife royalty, the panthers, even the eagles.

Florida inhaled change. It was in the air like the scent of salt and pine needles and orange blossoms and intriguingly stinking marshes, and like the smell of exhausts on the interstates. Change became a constant, a permanent part of its illusory impermanence, but a hindrance in the search for home and place. It meant that even among the familiar, there always was a rift and intrusion.

A sense of Florida should include and accommodate all that to be complete, but maybe nobody understands Florida completely, because Florida changes so fast. We know Florida the way we know next week's weather or tomorrow's arriving stranger. All of us are like the adventurous ones at the beach who always build another elaborate sandcastle, though knowing that the winds and the tides will wash it away. Florida is time and sand and water, pretty to see, easy to enjoy, pesky to capture. A sense of the place involves accommodation and respect. Understanding it becomes a pursuit, not an achievement.

Being at home in Florida means you find a way to belong, to fit, to feel attached and protective, wherever you live. Home need not be peculiar like the scrub, where I live. Each place has its own peculiar ambience to be discovered. If I can love the scrub, you can love a high-rise condo, or a city apartment, a grand mansion or model 1A in a subdivision. Whatever, it will be a piece of the mosaic that makes up Florida. When you find that you can laugh if your place displeases strangers, you are a Snowbird no more. You have found a home.

Mountains without Nosebleed and Other Marvels

Florida never had a real mountain, though it has tried hard to pretend. Most notably there was Iron Mountain (alt. 324.3 feet) near Lake Wales. It was believed to be the highest natural point in the state when Edward V. Bok bought it in 1929 and transformed it into a sanctuary centered by a beautiful marble tower and carillon that cost one million Depression-era dollars.

Bok Tower Gardens eventually became the most serene public place in Florida, another of those quiet havens that more tourists should visit, but it was hardly a true mountain. You could drive in comfort right up its gentle slopes. Worse, geologists discovered later that there was another place higher anyway, at a small community called Lakewood (alt. 345 feet) in Walton County, up near the Alabama line. So it goes in Florida. Every peak, natural or cultural or statistical, suffers the risk of being surpassed.

The closest thing Florida ever had to a locally practicing mountain climber was an elevator. Even in Georgia, there are basements whose altitudes top the highest natural peak Florida can offer. If man-made counted, the major harvests of the modern world—garbage and trash—

are being piled high enough in some fly-bitten and scavenger-plagued places to mount challenges (Mount Trashmores).

Lakewood, naturally, became a stop on my first swing around the state in 1973, and I returned many times. The first trip, though, remains the most memorable one.

An old railroad depot sat out in the middle of a cornfield, and the post office, where Mrs. Hazel Britton presided, had portholes. The building had been a boathouse on Lake Jackson up the road near Florala, Alabama, and the Brittons moved it to Lakewood. She served as postmaster from 1966 until her death in 1976, and after that Lakewood lost its post office.

Mrs. Britton was a charming lady who wrote poetry and devoutly believed in Lakewood. "I'll tell you how old I am if you won't tell it," she said. "I'm 85. Now don't you tell it."

I sent her a copy of the column in which the truth was revealed, and she was pleased. She wrote me a poem in appreciation and sent the clipping to her friend Robert Sikes, the congressman from her district. He inserted it into the *Congressional Record,* noting ceremoniously: "The American legend is comprised of much more than the big cities. . . . There are also the often untold stories . . . of the people in little towns and communities. . . . In these areas legends are born. . . . One of these worthwhile legends tells the story of Mrs. Hazel Britton." Mrs. Britton was an enterprising lady.

When the Brittons moved to Lakewood in 1904, they made it a company town for their lumber business. Fine forests and the coming of the railroad lured brothers Will and T. J. Britton, a pair of Scotsmen, down from North Carolina. By 1914, Lakewood had a depot, and steam locomotives ran on its 30 miles of spur track. There were two general stores and a commissary, a sawmill, workers' quarters, and all the trappings, including at the peak some 450 residents.

A milestone was the rising of the Lakewood Hotel, a three-story marvel for that time and place. "My, my," said one lady of that time, as the Brittons recalled it. "Three stories high and still in Walton County."

Depleted forests and the 1930s depression folded the lumber company and left a small historic community with mostly Hazel Britton's dreams of rising again. The railroad tracks were taken up. The state did put up signs celebrating the altitude, but people kept stealing them. The Brittons and the state took turns replacing them. Finally, with joint Britton and county financing, Lakewood Park was established to celebrate it as the highest point in Florida. My last visit, Brittons still lived in the area.

(Across Florida, marvels of geography or terrain occur frequently, though perhaps none with quite so distinct if precarious a claim to fame (geologists say there may be other places higher in Florida, yet uncharted; they are not sure) as Lakewood.

From the Borderlands, which neighbor Alabama and Georgia, diverse miracles and mysteries wend all the way down the state to the Keys. I visited and wrote about most of them. Not all can be revisited in one book. I pick a few and mourn that I cannot describe all. Especially memorable for me was the ridge country that rolls out like a great interior spine down the middle of the state, starting below Gainesville and Ocala and threading between Orlando and Tampa Bay. Always fascinating were the Everglades, the historic and scenic Indian River, all of South Florida, and the wondrous Keys. A recounting only suggests the range and nature of Florida's marvels.

The Borderlands remind us never to underestimate the significance of a line drawn in the sand. If North Florida anchors the Tropic of Cracker, then the Borderlands crown it. They are the cultural equivalent of a demilitarized zone separating the states, an area of enthusiastic Cracker preservation, where old times frequently are not forgotten, though in some cases maybe they should be.

On the underside of Alabama, memorable Gandyville and its name-sake patriarch, John O. Gandy, served as an admirable example of the exchange across the borders. John O., 105 years old when I talked with him, wore a handlebar mustache and a broadbrimmed black wool hat, Lee overalls, a shirt formally buttoned right up to his neck, and carried a cane. He would have looked right at home on a tintype.

At least 10 families in the area, about as far north and west as you can go and still stay in Florida, bore his name or blood. Born October 14, 1869, in South Alabama, he moved to Florida in 1915 and bought a 72-acre farm for $1,650. He had a simple explanation for the move. "I was hunting for a place that suited me better than where I was living," he said.

In 1972, by act of the legislature, his home officially became Gandyville, properly marked by green road signs. A weekly newspaper printed his picture, and his daughter complained without a smile that it made Papa look too old.

Gandy, good-humored and alert, said he had not shaved off his mustache since 1897 and offered a charming stream of explanation. "Me and a bunch of boys was going to a Fourth of July picnic. We all shaved 'em off. My wife was there. She wasn't my wife then, but she was later on. She says, 'Unh, unh, John, what did you do that fer?' I said, 'Do what?' She said, 'Shave off that mustache.' I said, 'Well, there wasn't nothing wrong in that,' but she says, 'Well, don't never do it no more.' And I ain't never did it again."

❡ Far east of Gandyville, the Okeefenokee Swamp filters across the heart of the Georgia Borderlands. Around it the sands are gray, the creek waters run black, the population thins out, and the wildlife remains authentically wild.

Along there, you cannot tell Florida from Georgia without checking for the boundary line. Trouble is, you cannot always find the line. This narrow sandwich of land might be the best living Cracker museum left in Florida.

In the Borderlands, remember, calling somebody a Cracker probably will be considered a compliment. The reference, informal but honorable, loosely means a native or perhaps just a Floridian attuned to rustic Florida.

All life has not been conquered and homogenized and plasticized in the Borderlands; it still comes out of the earth and must be sustained by the earth. The Borderlands retain that classic duality of the South, the surface simplicity of the ancient struggle between good and evil that takes so many forms: Southern hospitality vs. redneckism, religious conscience vs. militarism, extraordinary human caring vs. racism, devotion to old-fashioned honor vs. get-smart opportunism.

Elsewhere in Florida that duality might seem to splinter into multiple, interwoven, contradictory, seductive considerations that obscure fundamentals and create margins for argument, but not in the Borderlands.

There always have been question and controversy about that Georgia border. When King George II granted the Georgia charter in 1732, Georgia stretched all the way to the Pacific and included what is now Los Angeles, an unlikely start for both. Five surveyors spent four decades drawing the present line, and it wasn't confirmed until 1872. Even so, lawsuits quarreled over it for another 15 years. The crooked St. Marys River (the river meanders for 175 miles covering what a straight west-east line would reach in 65 miles) determines the easternmost part of the boundary.

A story told by old-timers argues that the border remained so uncertain during the 1850s that one year a family whose house straddled the line declared a child born there to be a Floridian, but a year later it changed its mind and presented another child born in the same room as a Georgian.

For most of history the border has been open, freely exchanging migrators and outlaws and shoppers and tourists. Real-estate prices go up on the Florida side, and to some sin seems more easily available on that side, but that of course depends on the individual appetites. Exchange traffic continues, varying at times among being loving, caustic, respectful, and derisive.

Wags sometimes called Jacksonville the Biggest City in South Georgia. The description was rarely appreciated as Jacksonville, with the St. Johns River curling through the downtown, developed the skyline and the ambitions of a metropolis. Equally disliked was the bittersweet compliment that described Fernandina Beach as Georgia Heaven, after development in the 1970s and 1980s transformed it into a nationally known resort. Nevertheless, old times hang on. On the Florida side the common fare grits still was labeled Georgia ice cream. The squeal of a pig was praised as Georgia music. So it went in the Borderlands.

The story of Boulogne typifies their up-and-down history. When I visited there in 1982, Frank Walker told me about it. At the time Boulogne, bunched up along U.S. 1 and against the south bank of the St. Marys River, had about 20 families, down from its historic peak of 30. He said the community was named for a French city, but he did not know why.

The Walker saga started in 1948. Though he grew up in Boulogne, Florida, it was later, as a merchant in nearby Waycross, Georgia, that he noticed that two major highways (U.S. 1 and U.S. 301) joined for about 17 miles from Callahan, Florida, to the river, and that a postwar travel boom was beginning. At Folkston, Georgia, (five miles north of the border), a no-wait wedding business drew steady traffic from Jacksonville and other points. All that, and there was no handy motel.

"Well," Walker said, summing up his judgment of the business potential, "I thought it was mighty good." He bought land on the Florida side of the river, where he estimated the value to be five times greater than that on the Georgia side. "Same land, but this side is Florida. That makes the difference," he said.

Walker startled everybody by building a quarter-mile long motel in Boulogne, the first air-conditioned motel between Folkston and Jacksonville, he said, one big enough to house every citizen of Boulogne, with room to spare for company. People around Boulogne called it the World's Longest Motel. "A lot of people said I was crazy," Walker remembered.

He had it figured. Walker called his friend Governor Fuller Warren and offered to donate six acres of land to the state—directly across from his motel—if the governor would put an official Florida Welcome Center there. The governor accepted.

"I done pretty good," Walker said. "I made a million dollars in 10 years. Lots of tourists, lots of new marrieds. By four every afternoon we were full. We'd rent those 72 rooms and not even have to turn the neons on."

In the early 1960s, Walker and some others decided Boulogne ought to be a city. The legislature agreed, and Boulogne incorporated. Then it was able to levy a small tax and qualify for cigarette tax revenues. Boulogne installed street lights from the motel down to the river. "Must have been 60 of them. It was beautiful at night. People'd see that and stop."

As one of the town's five councilmen, Walker reigned as judge of traffic court every Monday afternoon. "Some of 'em got greedy," Walker said of his fellow officials. Traffic arrests were Boulogne's only cash crop. The town's lone policeman hauled in so many speeders that a night policeman was added; arrests multiplied. Some of those nabbed began to complain that any speed was too fast. Boulogne became nationally notorious as a speed trap. Automobile clubs and tourists agencies put a red circle around it on the map and advised motorists to stay away.

When Judge Walker, contending he was embarrassed to be handing out so many $25 and $50 fines, began dismissing the accused, a political fight erupted. After the dust settled, Boulogne was de-chartered and its beautiful lights taken away. The community's lucky streak soured. Two interstate highways went up—I-75 to the west and I-95 barely 10 miles east— and took traffic away from U.S. 1. Even the marriage business dwindled. Walker sold his motel, and Boulogne faded.

Fernandina Beach (15 air miles northeast of Jacksonville), on Amelia Island at the mouth of the St. Marys River, had a more storied boom-and-bust history. Since the arrival of the Frenchman Jean Ribaut in 1562, eight national flags have flown there and all manner of men and enterprises—from statesmen and millionaires and shrimp fishing to pirates and thieves and pulp mills—have made it their headquarters. After each cycle, the island has struggled back to prosper again.

A long sweep of salt marshes and the Amelia River separate the island (13.5 miles long, two miles wide) from the mainland. At high tide, water seeps into those tall marsh grasses; when the tide drops, the mud flats seem to rise and the smell of the sea is strong. During spring, the tide rises as much as nine feet. The tidal action creates fascinating vistas as well as marine life.

Once, the island was promoted as "the fig culture center of the South." It did not work out. Another time, a promoter discovered prolific mulberry trees and pledged to use them to make Fernandina Beach a silk center. He brought in a few silkworms, sold some stock, and little was heard of the idea again.

In the 1920s the local chamber of commerce put out some literature about a dream to connect the Atlantic Ocean and the Gulf of Mexico by way of Fernandina Beach and the St. Marys River. It typified the old boom philosophy. "The Atlantic to Mississippi Canal will be built just as certain as Nehemiah rebuilt the walls of Jerusalem," the blurb said, "and in the day that it is accomplished, Fernandina will be the New York of the South."

From about 1875 to 1900, tourism flourished in Fernandina. Shipping, shopping and social life thrived. Steamers stopped on a weekly schedule from New York, and two luxury hotels were built to accommodate visitors. As many as 100 schooners docked at one time. The old cross-Florida railroad, from Fernandina to Cedar Key, built before the Civil War by David Yulee (one of Florida's first two U.S. Senators), carried visitors to other parts of the state. Fort Clinch, now a state park and tourist attraction, was built near the mouth of St. Marys River in 1847.

In the 1970s, Fernandina Beach decided to capitalize on its remarkable history and a 30-block area of downtown (later enlarged to 50 blocks) that included an almost unbroken string of late-1800s homes and buildings was placed on the National Register of Historic Places. Downtown was retooled with a 19th-century look, and since then the business cycle has been mostly boom.

(If Gandyville and Lakewood generated visions of old Florida in the western Panhandle, a short drive south of them quickly restored the tourist and condo ambience of resort Florida. Along a miraculously beautiful stretch of Gulf beaches, the prettiest in Florida, boom growth dazzled. The miracle of Destin set the pace.

Almost directly south of Lakewood, no more than an hour's drive away, Choctawhatchee Bay opens up on the map as a huge mouth of water that straddles the boundaries of Okaloosa and Walton counties. The Destin strip, a sandy peninsula between Pensacola and Panama City that has the characteristic beauty and vulnerability of a barrier island, puts a lower lip of beaches on that mouth. So attractive was the strip that it was transformed quickly from a fishing village to a seasonal resort.

In 1960, the Destin population totalled 600. The first high-rise condominium went up in 1971. In the 1980s Destin hit 12,000 permanent population, and the figure was rising. During July, visitors swelled the total to 28,000, and Destin boosters forecast 70,000 or more in years to come. The lovely dune profile along the beach changed to tall and sawtooth—Sierra Destin, a range of high-rises.

In those early years, Walton County property went from 15 cents an acre for upland timberlands to $60,000 a front foot on the Gulf. Freshwater supplies, sewage, transportation, and hurricane evacuation became problems. Destin, and therefore the Panhandle, finally had something in common with South Florida. It began to recognize that the great god Growth could inflict pain.

Some of the converts were surprising. Davage J. (Buddy) Runnels, Jr., a Mississippi boy whose family moved to Destin in the 1950s, when he was six, rode the Destin Boom to affluence. He grew up swimming and skiing in a Destin harbor as sparkling and clear as a jug of mountain spring water. At 21, he went into the real-estate and insurance business. In 1984, when I talked with him, he had a string of major accomplishments as a condominium builder. Yet Runnels was becoming skeptical of uncontrolled growth.

"For me, it was an educational process. I became keenly aware about six years ago," he said. When he, his wife, and three children went swimming in the harbor, for example, they found the once-clear waters turning muddy with pollution. "It really hit me then: Hey, we're destroying what we love about this place." That was not all. "We began to realize that the negative aspects of uncontrolled growth affected profitability. Customers began to demand environmental sensitivity," he said. Runnels joined the growth management advocates, citing the educational benefits of the South Florida example, where growth hit first and hardest, before its mixed blessings were fully understood.

One jewel of natural Florida, another true marvel, lies mostly intact in the woods about 11 miles south of Tallahassee—Wakulla Springs, the deepest (a 4.5 acre basin, 185 feet deep) and most powerful of Florida's 17 major springs. Local boast says it is the largest and deepest in the world. The springs bubbles up 600,000 gallons of sweet water every minute.

A beautiful old lodge and the springs as they exist now were the handiwork of a controversial tycoon, the late Ed Ball, a remarkable man who managed the DuPont empire in Florida. At Wakulla Springs, he carved out a place where nature and serenity could be enjoyed in convenience—a place wild, but comfortably wild. There, armchair sportsmen could savor the good life.

Ball personally bought the springs in 1931, during the desperate days of the Depression, for $50,000. After his death the state bought the property in 1986 for $7.5 million, with protective clauses built into the agreement to protect what Ball had wrought. Ironically, many conservationists and environmentalists around the state—some of them once at odds with Ball (one critic labeled the springs wildlife sanctuary as "Ed Ball's private zoo")—agreed that his enterprise preserved a beautiful piece of Florida.

A year before that sale took place, Gloria and I spent a few days there. My description:

Alligators lie around the far rim of the springs in a jungle setting, watching everything that moves—the egrets and the great blue herons flapping cautiously in the weeds, the exuberant leaps of the mullet. They watch, too, young vacationers sharing the clear, deep springs. The gators seem fascinated by daredevil boys who jump off a 33-foot diving tower and plunge into the water with an explosion of bubbles.

When one of the smaller gators, an eight-footer, edges out a bit and points its long snout toward a small platform in the shallow water where the kiddies play, it appears too interested for comfort. A guide, watching, cranks up a powerboat and scares it away.

Beware those eight-foot and ten-foot gators, someone explained. They are friskier and more adventuresome than the older ones. Still, despite the lethargic guise, a 12-footer can move startlingly fast. A great thrashing and frothing of water and rippling of waves make its sudden moves a fearsome thing to behold.

Lying out in the sun, the unblinking eyes and the monstrous proportions of a 12-footer give it the menacing personality of a reptilian King Kong, a lazy one that sort of slides along on its belly. Rather than going grabbing, it likely will lie there as unmoving as a black stone, waiting for something to get careless and come close. Then, a lightning switch of the tail and a clamping of those great jaws bring food.

Of all the fascinating things about Wakulla Springs and the fenced-in sanctuary that enclosed it, two dominated: a sense of the uncaged wild immediately at hand plus the faint, pleasure-accenting uneasiness that it brought; and the contrasting sense of ease and elegance delivered by the lovely old white lodge with the red-tiled roof.

The lodge looked down at the springs across a wide, nicely clipped lawn studded with giant magnolias and hickories. It sloped to a shore scraped clean into a bathing beach on the near side. Mornings and evenings, a fog gathered low over the cool springs waters. Millions of little wild creatures chirped and sang. Huge catfish cruised the bottom, munching marine flora. A tall chain-link fence, with barbed wire stretched across the top, then angled toward the springs, separating the beach and the lawn.

A helpful visitor pointed out that if someone wanted to keep unpaid admissions out of the springs, the barbed wire slanted the wrong way. The desk clerk, Bea Harvey, smiled. In 1985, she had been a springs employee for 23 years. "That's not for people. It's for gators," she said. "They like to crawl on the beach at night. The barbed wire keeps them from climbing over the fence and coming up on the lawn, where some of the guests go for walks."

Legends have sprung up around the springs, about the Indians, about mastodons whose teeth have been found in the spring, about the local claim that Ponce de Léon came here hoping that this was his Fountain of Youth. A museum on the grounds explored all those.

Ball built the lodge with the vision of a special resort in mind, not expensive but genteel, emphasizing Tennessee marble and high ceilings and a great stone fireplace in the lobby, establishing through architecture a grand ambience. The kitchen and dining room were conceived as gracious in the Southern style. The dining room's high ceilings, 10 chandeliers, and huge windows overlooking either greenery or the springs produced the right setting. Each dining chair was a rocker.

In the kitchen then, the cooks turned out pan-fried chicken, black-eyed peas, grits, corn bread and local seafood, including fried mullet. Outlanders could get recognizable food, including a special navy bean soup, but there was no question that this was Southern dining.

During the 1940s, when Ball was godfather to the Pork Chop Gang—a confederation of rural legislators and business leaders who insured that state government was friendly to their interests—would-be governors found it beneficial to announce their candidacies at the lodge. With legislative reapportionment and a surge in South Florida clout, that tradition ceased.

In the lodge, huge fireplace andirons and iron grillwork on the stairway featured great blue herons, ibises, and snowy egrets. The woodwork was southern cypress. A German artist painted Indian murals on the ceiling beams. Spanish tiles decorated the Moorish arched door to the porch, where great picture windows framed the springs scene. The lodge opened to the public September 1, 1937.

The 25 rooms, except for the old Ed Ball Suite (it cost more), were moderately priced in comparison with other resorts and with many motels. They had no television, except in the lobby, where a community set was available to all. Every telephone call from the lodge was long distance because there were no close towns. The lodge ran like a home, without garish signs or loud noises, not even background music.

Flowing out of the spring, the Wakulla River forms and flows a crooked trail south and east for 15 miles to the Gulf. Here, in everyman's dream of what a nice jungle should look like, some of Johnny Weissmuller's *Tarzan* films were made. About five miles down the river, just short of the first highway bridge, a chain-link fence stretched across the water, another controversial Ed Ball creation to preserve privacy. Once it was called "the world's most famous fence"—another local boast—and it remained the only such private barrier across a waterway in the state.

The river fence went up in 1941 after a favored springs gator—an 11-

foot, two-inch, 650-pound behemoth nicknamed Old Joe (later stuffed and mounted under glass in the lodge lobby)—was killed by "assassins unknown" in the dead of night. Along that three miles of river protected by the fence, an area where no tourists are allowed, limpkins ate apple snails, deer tripped out of the forest to the water to drink, ospreys and grebes and gallinules and anhingas and a hundred or more other birds browsed the natural kitchen. A cottonmouth moccasin curled around a cypress knee. Buzzards glided and circled, searching for the leftovers of someone else's victims. The air smelled fresh and damp. The dark river banks rose into a tree and jungle border, and overhead there was a channel of blue sky. About it all there was a bit of natural majesty.

In the late 1960s, Ball blasted and dredged the springs basin and a portion of the river to give his glassbottom and jungle-cruise boats more room to maneuver. He put in a concrete dock. Environmentalists howled, and Ball drew a lawsuit. They lost, and he countersued and recovered court costs. He did not lose many battles.

In 1984, up to 100 couples a year came to the springs to get married, especially during summer. They took their vows outside usually, on the lawn or under the gazebo, while picnickers gathered nearby under the big trees, and children splashed and swam, and the alligators watched.

In winter, elderly folk, with their binoculars and bird books, convened, taking long walks in the woods, sitting quietly on the porch studying the trees, taking boat rides down the river.

Ed Ball tailored Wakulla Springs to suit his tastes, and it suited the tastes of a lot of other people, too.

Across the storied Suwannee River and down the great ridge, with the coasts sliding off either edge of an elevated interior spine, the Tropic of Cracker trails south, fading before the human and geographic diversity of central Florida and picking up gloss as it reaches into the pastel cities of the subtropics and down to the Caribbean Keys that string away from the bottom of the peninsula like so many windblown teardrops. On either side, sheathing the peninsula, dynamic barrier islands shelter the coasts and provide spectacular oceanfront dwelling for those willing to accept its jeopardies.

Sparkling little towns up and down the ridge—Howey-in-the-Hills, Clermont, Lake Wales, Frostproof, Sebring, Lake Placid and others—attracted less flashy tourists and retained more of their original character than the highly pressured cities on the coast.

Ambitiously named Frostproof, a little off the main track even for ridge visitors, seemed typical when I visited there. Years earlier, it had been named Lakemont. A local story went that when the name Frostproof was proposed, one civic stalwart objected. "Not until hell freezes over," he declared. Hell remained frost-free, as far as anyone knows, but the town became Frostproof anyway, and as a matter of civic pride the name was defended as a description.

"We just don't accept frost," said Dan Ruhl, director of public works in 1977. "We don't go by the weather bureau." The name originated during the 1890s after two hard freezes hit Florida within a matter of weeks and devastated the citrus industry. Elsewhere, fruit froze and trees split to the ground. Joseph Washington Carson, a local citrus grower, toured the damaged regions and made the suggestion. "We've got the name for this place now," he said. "It's Frostproof."

Explanations varied. One had it that the elevation (110 feet) caused the heavier cold air to slide down the sides of the ridge. Others pointed out that Frostproof was far enough south (17 miles below Lake Wales) to miss the worst cold and had the added advantage of being on a narrow neck of land between the warming waters of lakes Clinch and Reedy. However, the town found there was more than one way to be frozen out. U.S. 27 shifted away from it and took casual traffic with it. Even though the old route, newly called the Scenic Highway (Alt. U.S. 27) still ran through Frostproof, the *Frostproof News* then regularly described it on page one as "the worst piece of federal highway in Polk County." Whatever, come freezes or not, the town proudly remained Frostproof.

❧ Over on the east coast, between Fort Pierce and Jensen Beach, there lies a swatch of land and water that illustrates how the splendors of Florida were created and what has happened to them. Maybe it does not have quite the significance of the Everglades, which protect the water supply for South Florida, or the startling uniqueness of the Keys, whose islands string together into a linear county, but probably nowhere else in Florida does so broad a range of native beauty and heritage occur nose to nose with urban demands.

Here, in southeastern St. Lucie and northeastern Martin counties, the temperate zone wilts before tropical influences, and abundant life reflects the variety of that environmental transition. An ancient dune, 30 to 80 feet high and roughly a quarter-mile wide, extends north-south for about 11 miles. The dune is part of a coastal ridge that once lined much of the east coast down to Fort Lauderdale. This was the highest, most spectacular stretch left when I took a look at it in 1985. In most other places, it had been chopped up for cities and roads and shopping centers.

The wind, the waves, the rise and the fall of the sea shaped this scene in sandy stair steps that begin in the ocean, rise a notch to Hutchinson Island, stretch beyond it and across the Indian River Lagoon, step high again to the peak of the big dune along the mainland side of the lagoon, drop down to a mini-Everglades known locally as the Savannas, and then level off toward U.S. 1 and peninsular Florida. The view amounts to a living museum. The parallel formations indicate how the area took shape.

Some 125,000 years ago the sea level was higher and the coast was underwater. As the sea level fell, a sandbar out in the ocean turned into what is now Hutchinson Island. A lagoon on the land side of that sandbar turned into the Indian River. An island on the west side of the lagoon turned into the landlocked high dune. Farther west, the dry saucer of land that might have included a beach filled with rains and became the swampy Savannas.

From atop that high dune, you could look east early in the morning and see the sun climb over the edge of the world, rising out of the ocean, then over the oleander bushes and orchid trees of condominium-studded Hutchinson Island, then over the palm-lined lagoon that is called the Indian River. The distance from ocean to dune was three miles.

From that same spot late in the day, you could look west and see the sun set, angling down across the piney woods and subdivisions in the distance, highlighting the wild Savannas (a half mile to a mile across) and the shy yellow blooms of the swamp-loving spatterdocks with brilliant reds and purples and blues and oranges. Summer rains connected the ponds in the Savannas, turning the wetlands into something resembling a river whose sweet water nurtured trophy black bass.

As the Savannas are not a real river, neither is the Indian River, but it had that popular character. The river then was a shallow (averaging three feet, except for the nine-foot-deep channel of the IntraCoastal Waterway), salty lagoon that extended some 125 miles from Titusville down the east coast toward Jupiter Inlet. In truth, it was more like a lake than a river. It touched five counties, and even then some 600,000 people lived on or near its shores. It had no current and limited ocean outlets that permitted tidal flushing action.

The combination of the Gulf Stream offshore, the climate range from one end of the lagoon to the other mingling temperate and tropical life, and the four freshwater streams feeding into the lagoon made it a marvelous if endangered marine hatchery. Scientists called it the most diverse estuary in North America (400 species).

Fine, infertile sugar sands, hot under the Florida sun, gave the dune a scrub character, like a desert between two rivers—one salty, one fresh. The western slopes retained patches of scrub, with windswept sand pines that looked like stressed Christmas trees, and scraggly growth; on the east side, fine homes went up over the years, with watered and fertilized lawns that sloped greenly to Indian River Drive and across it to the lagoon.

Captain Thomas E. Richards was among the first white settlers to invade this lagoon and its smelly swamps and heavy infestations of mosquitoes. Richards, a sailing man and shipbuilder from New Jersey, succumbed to the tales of a Florida paradise. With his two sons, he sailed first to Key West, purchased pineapple slips or plantings, and then returned with them to Hutchinson Island. In 1879, he built a chickee (thatched hut) on the island and experimented with pineapple farming. Soon, Richards shifted across the lagoon to the high ground of the dune and there started the area's first successful pineapple plantation. After he built a house, his wife joined him at the place he named Eden.

Sarah Richards Babcock, one of two Richards granddaughters who still lived on the dune in 1985, remembered some of it. The other was Mabel Richards Willmore. A third granddaughter, Amy Richards Nickerson, was visiting, and the three of them had fun reminiscing.

"Grandmother was a lady," Sarah said. "She wouldn't come down here until he [Captain Richards] built a house. She wasn't going to live in any chickee."

Other settlers and other plantations followed Captain Richards. "A little town started here at Eden. They had a church and a schoolhouse and a post office," said Amy.

"We had just about everything," said Mabel. "All the plantations had packing houses and they held dances in them. We had a little trolley that carried the crates of apples down to the dock to be shipped."

"The river was so clean we could see the bottom, and we had big clams and oysters and crabs and turtles and all the fish you could eat," Sarah added. "Mama always knew where she could find us—down by the river."

The sisters sometimes waded and swam across. They remembered the river when large numbers of wading birds strolled the shallow flats, when egrets made clouds in the sky, when ducks blanketed the river. Some of the men fished at night by holding bright-burning pine knots close to the water. When they encountered schools of mullet, the fish would jump into their boats. Fish, they said, were so plentiful the men could herd them up onto the beach.

The island was larger then, they said. The beach later eroded so much that they could see tree stumps out in the ocean. Captain Richards, they said, was among those who urged tycoon Henry Flagler to bring his railroad into South Florida, to speed up the shipping of pineapples. In 1894, the tracks were laid through the Richards property on the way toward Palm Beach. The sisters said Captain Richards died in 1902. The riverside trail across his property, oyster shells laid over dirt or muck, became scenic Indian River Drive.

Robert Goodbread's experience with the dune contrasted sharply. When I visited him at his home that same year, he was living near the wild savannas, but on the back slope of a dune he called Tick Ridge, where he had grown up. "Now they want to call it Mars Hill," he said. "I don't know who invented that, but I still call it Tick Hill." Sam Goodbread, his father, once farmed pineapples on the dune, and Robert helped him.

"They called it Tick Ridge because when they came out here ticks would get on 'em, like dog ticks, you know," he said. He also remembers swarming mosquitoes so thick that workers wore netting in the fields, and he remembers the heat, the sweat, the tiny sand gnats crawling through the netting and getting into his eyes. "Run you crazy," he said.

Tick Ridge, part of Jensen Beach in 1985, was created in the old days for the workers. No one else wanted it then. White folk preferred the other side of the dune, facing the lagoon, where they could dock their boats. "They put the darkies out here on Tick Ridge. That's what they called us, the darkies," Goodbread said. "If they got mad at us, they called us something else."

The Goodbreads came from White Springs, Florida, up near the Georgia line. Sam Goodbread first left there to go to Sanford and work on Henry Plant's railroad. Later he heard that he could earn a dollar a day on the pineapple farms near Jensen Beach, and so he followed his fortune south in 1896. "That beat the 75 cents he was getting up the state," Robert said. "Six days a week, 10 hours a day. Big money." Robert was one year old when he came to Jensen Beach.

Sam Goodbread farmed pineapples on the dune and raised beans on Hutchinson Island. On the island, he picked his spots carefully, planted the beans shallow to avoid saltwater, and picked them by hand. "Good soil but trouble there was saltwater," Robert said. "You had to know what you were doing. Got a horse or a mule and a hand plow. Plowed about six inches deep. Go deeper, and you hit salt and the beans would die. Plant in October, harvest in April.

"Pineapples, beans, and fishing, that's all we ever had," he said. "Plant the pineapples about 18 inches apart, almost on top of the ground. Put cottonseed meal and tobacco dust in the furrows. They'd get ripe in June. Put 'em on the boat to Titusville or ship 'em out on the railroad.

"I'd go barefooted. Shoes'd keep me back. I couldn't stand 'em. I didn't wear shoes until I was 13 years old. Sand could get hot. You think this is a tale, but I'd pull up a bunch of grass, step on it, keep stepping on it, pull up another bunch of grass and step on it. Keep that sand from burning you up. Start out there and see things dancing [heat waves]. We'd call 'em monkeys. The heat. Call 'em monkeys dancing."

Sam Goodbread acquired a patch of the dune and called it Goodbread Hill, plus 72 acres on the mainland and 33 acres on Hutchinson Island, Robert said, but he died young—before Robert was prepared to take it over.

"If he'd lived to be 15 or 20 years older, kept going like he was going, I'da been Mr. Goodbread," Robert said. "Wouldn'ta been old Robert, I'da been Mr. Goodbread. If I'd had the least bit of understanding about responsibility, I coulda carried on after he died. But I didn't know what in the world to do. I was running around and kept slipping and kept slipping and finally didn't have nothing."

Nematode infestations ruined the pineapple business, and competition from Cuban pineapples discouraged any revival. Robert went away for 40 years. "Working at anything I could get my hands on, mostly hotels," he said. "Then I came back here and built me a house, and now I'm sitting on it." He was living there on Tick Hill, which had turned into attractive real estate, a dignified old man remembering hard times and lost opportunities.

❧ The Everglades system, too large and significant and mysterious and beautiful to be called a swamp, dominates the natural life of South Florida. On the map, under all its separations and names (Everglades, Everglades National Park, Loxahatchee National Wildlife Refuge, Everglades Agricultural Areas, Big Cypress, Big Cypress National Preserve), it spreads across the southern end of the peninsula and becomes the watery heart and soul of the region.

Marjory Stoneman Douglas, who defined the Everglades as "the river of grass" in her classic 1947 book, became its inspirational angel. John Pennekamp, editor of *The Miami Herald,* earned acclaim as father of the Everglades National Park because his political clout was critical to the creation of it. Nathaniel Pryor Reed of Hobe Sound, assistant secretary of the interior for fish, wildlife, and parks under presidents Nixon and Ford, spent most of his life raging against the spoilers of it and organizing crusades to save it. A Miami landscape architect named Ernest Coe first had the idea for an Everglades park in the 1920s, and his obsession with it paved the way for others. Geologist Garald G. Parker in the 1940s described the workings of the Everglades to author Douglas and out of his explanations she fashioned her "river of grass" definition. Parker also identified and named the aquifers that stored South Florida's water. Until he came along, *aquifer* was an obscure and unpublished term coined by a Stanford University professor to describe underground reservoirs of porous stone. All of them were distinguished in their pioneering associations with the Everglades, but perhaps none was more devoted to study of Everglades complexities or did more in activist public crusades to preserve its treasures than Arthur R. Marshall.

Upon his death in 1985, Marjory Stoneman Douglas grieved that the Everglades had lost its "greatest champion." For 30 years, Marshall was a leading figure in virtually every major public battle to preserve the natural systems of Florida, but the Everglades always was the centerpiece of his concerns. Marshall called himself a theoretical ecologist, but the intensity and energy he applied to environmental causes earned him a reputation as a Cracker Quixote.

Marshall, a publicly fierce but privately sensitive and kind man, spent a half century developing his special vision of Florida. He saw it differently than many others. He looked at Florida's life-sustaining swamps and rivers and lakes, catching and hooding the water supply, and saw the environmental equivalent of a human blood system. He looked at the people who made the cities hum and flow and at the wildlife that graced the forests and the delicate scrub country, and he saw the equivalent of a nervous system.

He saw much more as well. His mind constructed intuitions into theories about how and why it all worked or did not work. He suggested remedies that were not quite like the remedies anyone else suggested, at least not until they had heard Marshall's view. His dogged pursuit of a trailblazing role lighted the path for some scientists but infuriated others, because the proofs and the formulas for his ideas had not yet been devised.

One theory dominated his work—that the healthy flow of water through the Everglades was the key to South Florida's well-being. During the many times I talked with him, he always prefaced any discussion of the Everglades with a reminder about how it used to be. "The pristine Everglades was a unique river system," he said in 1984 at his home near Interlachen in the scrub country of North Central Florida. "Its flow of water began in the chain of lakes of the Upper Kissimmee River Valley. In rainy season, those lakes rose, spilling their waters south into Lake Okeechobee. When Okeechobee rose, it spilled water south into the great floodplain of the sawgrass Everglades."

Marshall argued that a Kissimmee River that naturally meandered into Lake Okeechobee filtered the water, and that the slowly descending sheet flow across the Everglades replenished the aquifers and therefore South Florida's water supply. When the Kissimmee River was ditched and channelized, he said, it took away the filters. The sheet flow, he said, was affected both by that and by the levees in the Everglades. Before Marshall died, the state began moving toward putting the meanders back into the river. Marshall saw it as a great triumph and vindication for his ideas.

In a letter to me, dated August 11, 1983, he noted early the possibility that the Kissimmee might be restored, and he fairly bubbled at the prospect that his theories would be proven. "No one really knew if Einstein was correct [in his theory of relativity]—not even he was absolutely certain of its validity—until that [atomic] bomb went off at Alamagordo.

My bomb is the Kissimmee ditch restored!" he said, again revealing the evangelistic intensity of his beliefs. In his last phone call to me—in January 1985, about three weeks before his death, his voice weary and illness dimming his vigor—he put it all into words one more time. "There's something wonderful about nature if we just have the wisdom to see it," he said. The other heroes of the Everglades agree that he saw it brilliantly.

℘ Your first winter in South Florida is a marvel that marks you forever. It pleasantly upsets a lifetime of seasonal certainty. Winter chill holds no more terror than ice cream. Summer is another story. December begins an explanation of why Miami was nicknamed the Magic City, and March finishes it. It reminds you of the reasons Fort Lauderdale and West Palm Beach and Fort Pierce and Vero Beach, as well as Naples and Fort Myers and the Keys, swell with snowbirds.

My first winter there in 1955, Miami was less than half the size it later became, and looking back now it was surprising how many marks of the future already were on it. While North Florida browned its leaves and shivered in the cold, South Florida tanned and swam. Winter had fall's glow and spring's exhilaration.

Magic was the way all of it was, a place poised and expectant. The hotel lights shone like Christmas trees along Collins Avenue in Miami Beach and along Atlantic Boulevard in Fort Lauderdale. A breeze kept the flags flapping, as though there always was a distant storm brewing, putting an edge on things, promising happenings. Whatever might come later, the first South Florida winter made it seem so special that it would stay fresh in the memories of any who experienced it.

South Florida winters had a kind of sheen to them, acknowledging responsibility to nothing but pleasure, no bad points registered, only a glow that touched eveything. Hucksters peddled that natural magic, shamelessly tricked it up with neon and sequins and whatever else might glitter, but that seemed okay. There was plenty of everything then, and as long as we had the price it was worth the price.

The bright pastels of the buildings and the glare of the sun and the booming greenery gave it the look of a place perpetually in bloom. This was a heaven that permitted sin, a backyard tropics with a touch of the Bahamas and a splash of Cuba (later the splash would become more like a river), a little of everything except natural ice. Exotics flourished.

Miami thrived as a sort of colonial outpost, dipped in tropical tints, peopled largely by expatriates, especially from the Northeast. Along the beach, you could stroll from hotel to hotel on an evening's pleasure jaunt, drop in almost any door, listen to anyone from a B-girl to Preacher Rollo and his Dixieland band to a trio that included Sammy Davis, Jr., or maybe to some torch singer on Miami Beach leaning her microphone into the night, hoping Walter Winchell had joined the late-night crowd. Sinatra sometimes came to town.

Geography might have separated South Florida from the rest of Florida, but the ocean barriers to the south were little hindrance. In the 1950s it was easier and cheaper to fly to Havana than to Tampa or to Orlando. To Tallahassee was a major safari, but flights to Havana cost $26 round trip and left every half hour virtually around the clock. You could fly to Havana for dinner almost as easily as you could drive across town.

Miami Beach was a fairyland of neon and glitter, a winter escape for the wealthy and the glamorous. It had a down-home Las Vegas personality, minus casino gambling. You went to Havana for that. The underworld nurtured a sort of picaresque Damon Runyon image. The Roaring Twenties were a mini-rehearsal for the Exploding Eighties. Al Capone years earlier had come to escape federal heat, not the winter. Syndicates had warred over who should control the gambling, some slyly enlisting official help. The smuggling trade pushed aliens and whiskey and guns, and fertilized Caribbean intrigue. South Florida, with a hint of too-hopeful reverse pride, considered itself then to be an open territory for organized crime, where the godfathers came not to do business but to take a holiday.

While South Florida celebrated the annual Orange Bowl festivities on January 1, 1959 (Oklahoma defeated Syracuse, 21–6, in the first national color telecast of the football game), it did not seem possible that anything happening in Cuba could be more interesting or important, but that's how it turned out. Fidel Castro's revolution came to power in Havana that day, and neither Cuba nor South Florida has been quite the same since. A long row of Cuban dominoes began to topple.

In 1961, as night city editor at *The Herald,* I came to work daily at 1 P.M. One January day I arrived a little early to find the brass scrambling to find someone to send to Havana, where revolutionary fervor was creating a crisis with the United States. I volunteered and within an hour was on a plane to Havana. I remember my week there well, especially one symbolic scene that would prove to be historic for South Florida.

January 4, 1961, as the ferry to West Palm Beach pulled out of Havana Bay just after sundown, carrying 85 U.S. embassy staffers back home, a skeleton staff of 11 left at the embassy—working late, burning classified papers, and cleansing the building of secrets—flipped on all the lights in a farewell salute. There along Havana's Malecón the building blazed alight, visible far out into the Caribbean. Those leaving looked back and understood.

For me, a Yanqui staying behind, it was a sad moment. This was prelude, three months before the Bay of Pigs invasion. The storm was gathering official momentum. Because of Castro's demands, the United States had broken relations with Cuba, and the Stars and Stripes did not fly that Wednesday. Havana was preparing for invasion. Talk of war was open, emotional.

Barefoot militiamen dug trenches along the Malecon and pointed 85-millimeter Czech-made artillery pieces north toward Florida. At the foot of the Prado, that tree-lined promenade, there stood a brace of 12.7-millimeter antiaircraft guns, also Czech-made. The players were posturing. The future was uncertain. Eisenhower, a Republican, a senior-citizen war hero, a Texan, was President. Kennedy, a Democrat, a glamorous young politician from Massachusetts born to wealth, would be inaugurated in 16 days.

Cuba had been turned upside down. Loyalty to the revolution superceded training and experience. Revolutionary fervor ran highest either in the rural countryside or among the young, bracketed from ages twelve to twenty-four. The military filled the city with rural soldiers. Girls of high school age and boys as young as twelve, part of the militia, manned machine guns. They were anxious.

No one on the street had any guarantees. Arrests were frequent and showed little pattern. They included Cuban officials and U.S. businessmen and U.S. newsmen (not me, fortunately) and any innocents brave enough to be too curious.

"Nobody will bother you as long as you observe the letter of the law," a friend at the U.S. embassy advised. "Of course," he added with a half smile, "the law changes every day."

U.S. Consul Hugh Kessler offered an interesting perspective. "When

John McMullan [an editor at *The Herald*] called to say they were sending someone over here, I advised him to make it someone expendable," he said. McMullan knew how to make you feel good about your work.

A Yanqui on the streets of Havana that week, accustomed to Cuba's pre-Castro old world courtesies and tourist pampering, found himself a pariah. He provoked suspicion, even fear. In speeches, the flamboyant Castro spoke frequently of invasion. On the radio, monotoned Che Guevara sounded like an excited undertaker. The newspaper *Revolución* carried blockbuster invasion headlines. Speculation and rumors were so constant that reports and counter-reports became disinformation. They served to confuse. Whether that reflected a purpose or reality was another speculation.

The invasion did not come until April, about three months after I had returned to Miami, hitting the south coast instead of the north, but it harmonized with the prelude. The fighting itself was a semi-secret hurrah, cloaked in propaganda and exaggerations, neither its tragic nor heroic aspects fully appreciated.

In Miami and the United States, reporters covered the three-day war long distance—via shortwave radio, via press releases from a New York public relations firm, via interpretations of Cuba's broadcasted boasts and complaints—and with more confusion than accuracy.

Until afterward, only the shooting participants had clear knowledge of the details. Some of their stories, even then, had to be screened for bitter emotions and scapegoating, much of it generated by the issue of whether the United States had betrayed the invasion by promising air cover and failing to deliver it.

I covered the Bay of Pigs invasion from the old Myrtle Bank Hotel in Kingston, Jamaica, if you can call that coverage. My job was to wait and be ready for a chance to enter Cuba behind the expected-to-be triumphant invaders. I passed the time sharing maps and speculation with Cuban exiles, listening to the CIA's Radio Swan issue last-minute cryptic messages and sabotage instructions to sympathizers or underground operatives, who, even if they heard, had little opportunity to respond inside garrisoned Cuba.

"The moon is red; the fish are running," the radio would announce.

There were radio instructions for all Cubans to take their phones off the hook at a certain hour in an effort to jam Havana communications, to turn on all electrical outlets hoping to short-circuit power sources, to throw tacks and broken glass on the streets, to put sugar in the gas tanks of military cars, or pull engine wires loose.

Then, more swiftly than anyone expected, it was over. Most of the invaders became prisoners. Rather than being overthrown, Castro was strengthened. Eulogies by historians called it a perfect failure.

Repercussions began. The flow of Cubans escaping to Florida accelerated. Crisis after crisis followed (including the big one, the Cuban Missile Crisis of October, 1962, when Miami feared war might reach its own city limits). I had a good look at it all, from both ends. In 1964 and 1965, as Latin America Editor, I spent a total of about 10 weeks in regimented Cuba (including five hours with Fidel Castro on Halloween night, 1965, at Varadero Beach, in the company of three other reporters). In the late 1960s and early 1970s, as an ivory-towered editorial writer, I saw things close-up as the new Miami, with a strong Hispanic influence, began the process of blossoming into an international city. Extraordinary blessings, new vigor, and new visions mixed with cultural and ethnic conflicts; the ferment began producing something special.

The future, when it arrived in the 1980s, proved to be not so much a departure from character as an uneven growth among the parts. There was a shift in muscle and prominence. Fantasies exaggerated the old chemistry, frightening some but fascinating more. The appeal graduated to be futuristic, hallucinogenic, and it perfectly fit the times that had arrived.

Civically dismaying wrenches of crime and politics salted into rocket-like bursts of achievement. They were accented by discoveries of shocking neighborhood pockets where yesterday's problems worsened without civic interference.

Miami evolved into the City Surreal, the home of the unexpected, a place that juxtaposed opposites and suffered nationally from dangerous reputation. No more was it a serene place in the sun, where the elderly dozed away the winters with relative assurance that the wackos would not intrude. It had turned young and reckless again. It became a place where you needed speed and balance to keep up.

The with-it crowd's finger-snapping performances transformed that old stage, the backyard tropics, into a new sensation. Miami, without a blush, adopted a TV melodrama—a live comic book—as its favorite promotion. The show snapped, crackled, and popped like a modern child's cereal, full of action and sweetened to taste.

Miami Vice stressed South Florida's underworld lining, even reflecting some of its truths, and Miami dug back into its past for that old reverse pride and approved. *Miami Vice* took those original pastel colors and booming greenery and enhanced them with creative juices and contrasts. The rest of Florida snickered that a city so sensitive to its civic problems would hail the television show as though it were soul theater. They did not know that this did, indeed, represent the evolution of Miami soul.

Nothing so strange about that. In the backyard tropics, the exotic catches on easily, and flourishes. Life swells and booms and begins again. The players have international scope and talent and resources, and there are feathers of inspiration in every breeze. Eccentrics, earnest homesteaders, smiling predators, blinking Snowbirds, puzzled Crackers, ensnared strangers intending only to pass through, ministers of sunshine elbow among the stars. It was like repertory theater, where the show changed but not the basic ingredients that produced it.

The geography, the big sky, the flat land and the wide ocean, coupled with the exotic plants and their equivalent in people, suggested deceptively that South Florida was only a class recess, playtime. Nothing really counted. Rules were suspended. You could be a little crazy, if you wished, and it was all right.

That ambience masked the realities of subtropical life for the mass of South Floridians, who might have had a better stage than much of the rest of the nation but still had to work and worry like everyone else. Moreover, sweating through six-month summers that radiated reality, they fretted about crime and politics while resenting their city's reputation for those things.

Visitors dubbed Miami the New Beirut, Casablanca, Havana II, Marseilles, Babylon, Last Frontier, City of the Future. They strained to find an explanation for South Florida somewhere else, in some other pattern or place, and none fit precisely. It was an original.

◊ At the bottom of Florida, beyond the water's edge, there is still another marvel—the Keys, the Conch Republic. Thirty-five bony little islands strung off the tip of South Florida and curved west, forming Florida Bay as they stretch 130 miles to the end of the road, Key West.

Going into the Keys was not merely a visit; it was an immersion. Sunlight and broad vistas laid a thick presence on you, something less than water but something more than thin air. The nostrils whiffed that natural Keys smell, the thick and oddly pleasant scent of mingled salt air and seaweed and fish residue. It induced the brain to drop into low gear. Horizons opened wide, sunlight intensified to a white glare, jewellike blue and green waters took on a hypnotic glitter, and sunrises and sunsets bewitched anyone with warm blood. The weather and the sea toasted you and then salted you, as though you were a peanut, and it made you feel delicious.

The Keys, barely holding their heads above a deepening Caribbean sea, created a marvelous illusion: a mountaintop experience at sea level. Just wide enough to sheathe a highway, necklaced by bridges into something unique, they reached their highest altitude of 18 feet at Windley Key while averaging less than five feet high.

Naturally beautiful, extraordinarily vulnerable, they comprised national treasures that historically relied more upon the restraint of strangers than upon restrictive rules to determine how they grew and developed. They belonged in the rank of the Grand Canyon and Yosemite and the Everglades as places of natural wonder, but they were a thing even beyond those. You could see most of the Keys, the most spectacular view in Florida, from a car while driving over that sierra of bridges. At the John Pennekamp State Park, glass-bottom boats showed you a living coral reef. At a state park on Windley Key, the sheared walls of an old coral rock mine dissected petrified reefs and helped explain how the Keys came into existence a thousand centuries ago. The Keys, accessible to everyone of almost any age and health, were the essence of oceanic Florida.

Had the Grand Canyon and Yosemite been so hospitable to whatever came as the Keys have, it would have been decried as a national disgrace. But in the Keys a natural heritage that money cannot reconstruct has been cut up and sold for inflated dollars, and some have hailed it as progress.

The Keys operated for years as though they were paradise with an open admissions policy and forgiving laws. They had welfare zoning that benefited wayfaring strangers at the expense of local residents. Rising taxes, strained public services, and uncertain transportation complicated ordinary lives. Traffic smothered the ease of access to that spectacular view. The smallest emergency threw the single main highway, U.S. 1, into a hopeless snarl. Costs of living led the state, forcing out old-timers accustomed to living on the economic edge and closing down the colorful if tacky little mom-and-pop businesses.

Over the years growth fastened upon growth, like elegant clusters of oysters piling one upon the other, each advertising the possibility of a pearl within, each diminishing if not tainting the old Keys. Pollution threatened the coral reefs and endangered the once royal fishing. As a hurricane escape route, the prospects became scary. The zoning had religious overtones: so meek and so humble that it blessed and forgave almost any sin. Drinking water was pumped from mainland Dade County's well fields, where Miami already worried about whether it had enough and was supplemented by desalinized sea water. Under a crush of development, the Keys slowly evolved into a linear city, an urban spine lacking enough land for the usual flesh and variety, ever more dependent. It was like looking into the human mirror and despairing at the frailty viewed there.

As always in Florida, it was a delicate balancing act: how to grow and prosper without uglification. In human terms, it was the exceedingly difficult problem of mustering courage and grace enough to cull and utilize the wisdoms of age without being turned cranky by the pains and losses. Maybe no one could do it as well as he would like.

My many trips to the Keys during the 1980s persuaded me that the Keys were pigging out on growth, overtaxing their limited resources and space, forcing costs up and quality down for permanent residents, selling away an old insouciance that money could not reconstruct, and turning into a bohemian facade—fodder for poseurs, messages for T-shirts—no more real than Disney World.

Old Conchs (natives, the term deriving from a local shellfish) steadily were being squeezed out. People who knew the Keys best—who understood the old Keys philosophy of tolerance, of accepting human quirks with grace—were abandoning the rocky islands to pretenders with a weakness for pseudo-Conch posturing that transformed what once were the necessities for survival into a self-conscious mimicry. Going barefoot and ragged could be honorable and honest, or it could be the equivalent of wearing Mickey Mouse ears a decade or so beyond an age when it might be amusing. Still, real Conchs survived among the fakes.

〔 Wilhemina Harvey, who officially made me an Honorary Conch in 1982, was the Big Mama of Keys politics, the Queen Conch. Since 1832, five generations of her family had lived in Key West, and she was the third generation born there. She had a long background of civic involvement and knew the sensitivies of her fellow Conchs as well as anyone else. She was the first woman elected to the Monroe County Commission since the county was founded in 1823. She was the first woman chosen as county mayor. Her husband, C. B., once had been mayor of Key West. With pleasure she related the joke going around that they had Her Honor and His Honor towels in the bathroom, rather than just His and Hers. By 1984, she had emerged as a politician who cared about human problems. She was a lady in the old-fashioned sense as well as a woman demanding her rights. When treated discourteously in political wars—some suggested she was a flighty woman—it won her public sympathy.

Having lunch with her at Key West's Pier House was an experience. The entire room was under her eye and nod. She presided. People called to her. She waved, she smiled. She did not have time to eat. She was Wilhemina the wonderful, who loved everybody and wanted everybody to love her, and she had a good batting average. At 72, she reigned and bubbled, a matriarch who could still giggle.

"I don't know whether I'm the most influential [politician in the Keys]," she said discreetly, "but I'd like to think I'm the best loved." The previous fall, she had been dumped as county mayor, turned into a martyr, and had come back stronger than ever. Three male votes turned her out. "A diabolical plot," she called it. She had been baited and harassed before. Once, a commissioner called her an idiot. Mad, she retaliated politically and in the next election got a more favorable balance on the commission.

"This year, for the first time in many years," she said, thinking it over carefully, "I think we'll have a commission that votes on the merits of the issues, . . . not because if you do something for me, I'll do something for you. That's a big change."

Wilhemina, the Big Mama of Keys politics, at least that once taught the bad boys a lesson. In summing up that experience, noting that for a change the commission would be voting on the merits of the issues, she summed up Keys politics.

In the Florida Keys, everything seems wonderfully possible. Wonder and surprise lace the extraordinary beauty and give it an appealing dimension. Rats climb palm trees, stores brag about offering "Miami prices." Escapists flock to the Keys but have to congregate near the nation's No. 1 highway, an oceangoing Main Street. Prized little Conch houses, crafted by boatbuilders, sit ear to ear on tiny Key West streets, while old-timers decry the new concepts of cluster housing.

The world-class Keys, an enduring international attraction masquerading as backcountry, are half ocean, half island, half city, half rural—and the rest is original rock and reef. That amounts to too much? Exactly.

From Lakewood at the top to Key West at the bottom, Florida unreels marvel after marvel like an unending book that spins out chapter after chapter and entices you to keep exploring.

The Fruits of Charm

Nostalgic laments of old-timers about the Florida wonders of years past—giant oysters, panthers that shrieked in the night like women in pain, deserted beaches and dunes unbroken mile after mile, bays frothing with fish, thousands of wading birds stalking the estuaries, gulf and ocean waters as clear as a mountain spring, towering forests and silent swamps—refresh awareness of Florida's natural heritage, but their tales grow thin. As time and consumption erode the natural charms, Florida needs better ways to keep alive its truths.

Along with conventional parks and preserves and sanctuaries, it needs individually inspired memorials of the beautiful places, reminders that stand up like witnesses in court. It needs public examples: here is how Florida was, and this helps explain the nature of this place and how we ought to harmonize with it. It needs place obituaries that recall rare, lost places so that unaware new Floridians, as well as forgetful older ones, can know what was and can gauge the significance of change, make judgments, raise intelligent questions about what constitutes progress. It needs examples and benchmarks that keep baseline data on beauty warm in the emotions of its prime time. It needs accounts that tell us conclusively about a place, what happened to it, and to what purpose. It needs to keep handy the conclusions of experience so that the accuracy of hindsight will not be wasted, so that its lessons may be applied to whatever beauty and value remain.

Once, auto safety officials planted crosses along the highways to mark the sites of fatal auto accidents. The idea was to suggest how routine but close rode the reality of death on the highways. In Florida, we need a continuing public alert of some kind for the fatal accidents that can happen to the natural treasures.

Extraordinary springs like this one here, beaches and shorelines like this, houses like this, marine life like this, once were common in Florida. Or, something wonderful existed on this very spot, a place obituary might say, but it was killed by these circumstances and for these expected benefits and here is how it turned out. This would be local history in its most powerful form. Here under this black asphalt parking lot with its yellow security lights there once stretched a wetlands where roseate spoonbills splashed. Once a wind-rippled sandhill where Floridians walked barefoot stood here under the pancaked concrete of this shopping mall. For pictures and full testimony, cross-indexed, go to the library.

Here was a reef or a river or an estuary or a mini-Everglades that died because somebody decided that the more profitable use was for a condo, or an expanded marina, or a convenience store; the zoning and growth management authorities approved. Looking back now, were they right? Does the perspective of time confirm the judgment? Was a beautiful place traded for something worthwhile? If the natural place were still here, what impact would it have on the area's quality of life and on its business prospects?

Maybe it would not change anything. Maybe tomorrow's planning always will turn on the simple, blind appetite for more, for always rising numbers. Maybe there are no unstretchable limits. Maybe numbers as philosophy bring the right emphasis to our lives. Maybe, but to me it does not seem so.

Hazel Britton so loved the high ground of Lakewood that finally it was recognized with a county park. Ed Ball so loved Wakulla Springs that he preserved it, and out of his efforts at memorial came a park. Edward Bok so loved Iron Mountain that he created Bok Tower and endowed a private foundation to preserve it. Ding Darling, the conservationist and cartoonist, so loved Sanibel Island that a wildlife sanctuary there perpetuates his passion and bears his name. The string goes on. The examples are plentiful. Charm has a flaw—it invites consumption—but it also creates a love that preserves. The fruits depend upon how we utilize the charm.

𝄐 Consider Windley Key, once called Umbrella Key, a rocky little island at mile marker 85.5 (bayside) whose history helps explain the mysteries of the Keys. The rescue of three old limestone quarries there tells the best side of the Florida story—how, in a state teetering for balance, the commitment of one or a few can tilt the whole thing.

The quarries propelled a multi-talented, hardheaded church organist into politics, and out of that came a unique state park, officially titled the Windley Key Fossil Reef State Geologic Site. Alison Fahrer, a grandmother and the organist at Plantation Key's St. James the Fisherman Episcopal Church, had a sweet smile and enough grit to blunt a diamond drill. She had a lot of help, but in the beginning almost no one but her believed the old quarries could be saved.

Fahrer, originally from Spokane, Washington, bought a vacation home on Windley Key in 1960, just one month before Hurricane Donna destroyed it. Typically, she rebuilt a nicer place. After 13 years as an executive with the Baldwin Company in Cincinnati, in 1977 she and second husband, William G. Fahrer, Jr., an advertising man, returned to Windley Key to live. Their home sat sandwiched between two high-rises on an ocean cove across U.S. 1 from the old quarries, which at the time were idle, inaccessible, and uninteresting to most of the public. Both the Fahrers were accomplished musicians and stout Republicans entering a Democrats' den.

Windley Key originally had been homesteaded in the 1800s by Benjamin and David Russell, Keys pioneers. (In the 1990s, their great-great-grandchildren attended local schools.) In 1908, the Russells sold their property to the Florida East Coast Railway for $852.80 at a time when Henry Flagler was pushing to extend that railroad all the way down to Key West.

The railroad quarried stone from Windley Key to help lay the foundations. Workers drilled holes deep into the coral rock and used dynamite to shear away huge slabs, leaving walls that looked like stone murals. The patterns revealed coral reef life as though seen from the inside—great fans and intricate swirls and curlicue formations made by growing reefs that had fossilized after the sea receded during the ice ages.

Following the finish of Flagler's railroad in 1912, and until as late as the early 1960s, workers quarried and shipped out the rock—sometimes called Keystone—for use as decorative facade for buildings. The Deering estate, the Miami public showplace called Villa Vizcaya, used it.

After the work stopped, scientists used the quarries as an educational tool. They called it "the other half" of John Pennekamp Coral Reef State Park (Key Largo headquarters at mile marker 103). Students looked at the living coral reefs at Pennekamp Park and then stood inside the quarries and saw dissections of the fossilized reefs. "A comparison of the two constitutes an absolutely unique system for the understanding of all the important coral reef environment," said Dr. Cesare Emiliani, chairman of the department of geology at the University of Miami. "Nowhere else in the world can the geologist stand within a petrified coral reef."

In 1972, the university queried the FEC about preserving the tract but was put off. Even though a rush of development came to the Keys during the 1970s, the quarries appeared safe in railroad hands, as well as being protected by zoning. Late in 1979, though, there came a surprise. The quarry property, 32.88 acres from U.S. 1 to the bay, had been sold to a developer via a swap of Duval County land the railroad wanted. It was tax-appraised at $316,000. The developer bought it on speculation that he could get the zoning changed (a good bet in terms of Keys history), and planned to put a $10-million, 156-unit condominium development on it. One quarry would be turned into a tennis court, the others converted into kayaking ponds.

Alison Fahrer, with other Keys conservationists, early in 1981 began a quarry crusade. An ad hoc committee formed, drawing representatives from all the Keys (in all, eventually, 1,200 people and 25 organizations), with Fahrer at the head of it. The zoning board approved the condos (tripling the tax-appraised value of the property). While a developer's representative ridiculed their opposition, the committee plugged on. Politics was the problem. Fahrer made a decision. Fellow conservationist Ed Kloski, a Middle Keys builder, replaced her as head of the committee and she ran for county commission.

"I got into the campaign because the zoning board treated us as if we were utter fools and frauds," she said.

Fahrer won by one (yes, one) vote, becoming the first woman Republican ever elected to the county commission, and proceeded to distinguish herself as a well-prepared, determined, pragmatic commissioner (for one term, losing narrowly in a re-election bid). During a year or more of stormy hearings about the state's mandated land-use plan for the Keys, she kept the quarry issue before state officials. Kloski and the coalition of civic groups kept hammering away, too. Finally, after years of persistence, they won. In 1985 the state bought the quarry acreage for $3.2 million to create the park envisioned. Later, it would enlarge the plan to include a two-story building—the Alison C. Fahrer Educational Center—that could be used as a hurricane refuge of last resort (taking advantage of Windley Key's 18-foot altitude, highest in the Keys). A Florida Department of Natural Resources official put state appreciation on the record. "Without Alison Fahrer," he said, "there would have been no park."

Fahrer and friends won a big one. So did Florida.

All the battles have not been so neatly concluded, even when successful. One occurred about 17 miles south of Windley Key, beginning in 1954, when Russell Niedhauk and wife, Charlotte, settled on Lignum Vitae Key, a true island on the bayside of Lower Matecumbe. There was no bridge. There, with Don Quixote zeal, they entered the realm of Keys legends.

In Old World style, Russell Niedhauk's father had apprenticed him as a teenager to a Pennsylvania steel mill. Work there seasoned, tempered, and forged Russell, who reached a personal altitude of five feet, four inches, into a man upon whom convention might splash but could not dampen, a man destined to attract bureaucratic lances and then break their pointy noses.

When his father moved to Florida for reasons of health, Russell went with him. The young man worked on a towboat that operated on the New River Canal between Fort Lauderdale and Lake Okeechobee, became a licensed radio operator, a machinist, an engineer, a naturalist, a woodworker, a mechanic, anything he needed to be. He could make almost anything, repair almost anything, identify almost anything alive.

Russell married Charlotte Arpin in 1926. They lived as caretakers for two years on isolated Elliott Key, an island in Biscayne Bay north of Key Largo. After the monster 1935 hurricane raked it clean, they moved and eventually found their way to Lignum Vitae, again as caretakers. They lived on that isolated, privately owned 280-acre island for 21 years.

By the time I talked with the Niedhauks in 1981, they had moved onto a 65-foot houseboat tied up at Islamorada. He was 79 then, a tiny Germanic man with a thick head of gray hair who peered at you through glasses any mad scientist would admire. The physical dimensions seemed inadequate for containing so large a spirit.

With his faithful wife, Charlotte, alongside—"Hush, Charlotte," he would say with that deceptively sweet cordiality. "Don't butt in for a minute"—he explained in proper chronology and precision how he became addicted to the isolation and unique beauty of Lignum Vitae.

Though he had little formal training, by instinct and curiosity and perseverance he became a source of information that scientists and historians courted. On Lignum Vitae, he discovered a beetle—a Coleoptera, about a half-inch long and with pretty grayish and brownish and yellowish colors—which was named for him, the Niedhauki. Once, a picture of it graced the cover of *Natural History* magazine.

Niedhauk's unusual experiences included sitting on the bottom of a south Florida canal and feeling the saltwater flowing inland—while across the top of it a swirl of lighter freshwater flowed out to sea. He was an early forecaster of the water disaster that threatened South Florida unless the canals were closed and salt intrusion slowed. Niedhauk had learned to predict the arrival of hurricanes, he said, by observing the movements of marine creatures.

His explanations made it sound as though the harmony of the environment and the Niedhauk personalities was so special that it attracted the jealousy of the gods and their government minions. A joust of Olympian proportions took place between the Niedhauks and the state, all of it within the microscopic focus of Lignum Vitae.

The problem developed because the Niedhauks had an oral promise that they could continue living on the island, and the state wanted them off. Naturally, Russell and Charlotte, as is required of legends, fought Florida to a compromise, but the argument went back and forth for a long time—first the state winning, and then the Niedhauks winning, and then neither winning—and it was an unsatisfying thing. Petitions circulated in the Keys supporting the Niedhauks, and prominent personalities deplored the divorcing of them from Lignum Vitae.

Finally, it ended, or subsided. A lawsuit resulted in an official compromise. After four years of bickering, the Niedhauks first moved onto their boat and docked it off the island. After three years of that, they moved it to a marina at Islamorada.

The hurrah was all over, Niedhauk said. The controversy had washed away. He and Charlotte lived on their big boat with the seven-foot-high ceilings and seven-foot-long bunks and grieved about their lost island. They felt forgotten. Russell, at 79, took a skiff over to Lignum Vitae five days a week and stayed four hours a day, maintaining the machinery there as he always did, still cataloguing flora and fauna in ways that in the old days had excited scientists from at least three universities, still literally nursing his beloved island for the federally set minimum wage. To him, the personal loss seemed immense.

Neighborhood dogs routinely scrambled aboard their boat to find the cookie jar maintained for them. They talked with their "double-yellow" parrot. Visitors dropped by to admire Russell's woodwork and the family antiques they had managed to save. Charlotte sprinkled bee pollen granules on their salads as preventive medicine for allergies.

The Niedhauks thus passed into the legends of the Keys, warriors for the special place they loved, instruments in bringing it recognition and preservation, their memories special but bittersweet.

◊ Florida feeds and grows upon perpetual, restless movement and change. Maybe no other state has such significant tides and countertides. It is the home for nomads, where beans grow in the winter, where whatever dream that can be conceived can be peddled, where millions eagerly migrate to revel in the Florida dream without committing to it as home. Florida lends itself more easily to a sense of ownership than to a sense of belonging.

Human tides flowing this way and that bring swells of energy that make everything work. Parts of the Florida population are like restless crew members who jumped off the legendary *Flying Dutchman,* freed from the curse of being forced to roam forever but unable to make up their minds in paradise, shuttling up and down the peninsula making and unmaking decisions. The ever-rising population (less than one-third native), the Snowbirds and tourists, the refugees, the migrating workers, Floridians moving about within the state keep the pot boiling and the real-estate salespeople happy.

Enjoying charm requires focus and time. Some of Florida's wisest voices have talked about that. "A lot of Floridians haven't been here long enough or had a chance to think about it enough to really make this state a part of themselves. It is this business of not yet thinking of Florida as home, not developing enough of that feeling of caring about it. It's a much deeper problem than many realize," said Victoria J. Tschinkel. We talked often while she was head of the Florida Department of Environmental Regulation. In 1984 she began pushing the idea of citizen commitment to Florida. "We need to get together in this state, develop this sense of a Florida character, and reflect it through our government," she said.

Julie Morris had a similar answer. She was a quiet sort, but she nevertheless ranked as a full-fledged doer, a dedicated feminist, a committed conservationist. In the 1980s, she and husband, Jonathan Miller, coordinated the environmental studies program at New College in Sarasota. Their consulting business assisted four Florida counties with comprehensive land-use plans and did research on the rivers and barrier islands of southwest Florida. During her first five years in the 9,000-member Sierra Club of Florida, she served two of them as conservation chairman and another two as general chairman, the principal officer. She contributed in a public capacity as a member of both the Florida Coastal Resources Citizens Advisory Committee and as a director of the Florida Game and Fresh Water Fish Commission.

Morris, who fled Wisconsin for Florida in 1970, had a quality sometimes missing from young and dedicated environmentalists—a thoughtful temperament that resisted being provoked into radical postures. She preferred to persuade rather than to badger, but she could strike sparks without using flint.

"I love Florida," she said when I talked with her in 1985. "I'm thoroughly bonded to it. But when I go visiting back North, the people who know me can't believe there's a Florida that someone like me can love," she said. "Their impression of the state is that it's a kind of walled highway experience—rinky, tinselly, a selling-itself kind of thing. New Floridians encounter that. They see the stereotype of what Florida is, and they have a hard time getting beyond that. There's no easy way to get acquainted with the cultural or natural heritage of the state. So many don't fall in love with the real Florida for a long time, maybe never."

It is not always easy but many do find their place and make their commitment, like the Fahrers and the Niedhauks, or the Balls and the Boks and the Darlings. They make a difference, even though sometimes their contribution is quieter and more personal. They choose their place and stake out their home. Their families and homes blend into place, maximizing both themselves and their surroundings, creating respect in their neighborhoods encouraging others to do the same. They serve Florida well.

The Morgan family came down from Tennessee in the 1930s. They put together some rural acreage near Payne's Prairie, not far from the ancient village of Micanopy, and sank their roots deep into North Central Florida. In 1939, they planted 44 orange trees. If you lived in Florida, you wanted orange trees. They were proud of the trees, and the oranges tasted good. Maybe they looked a little rusty, but they squeezed out juicy and sweet.

Time passed. The first generation of Morgans died, but the next generation took over; still another, the third generation in Florida, began to apprentice in the Morgan ways. The land, eventually reaching about 100 acres, became a family compound, with sons and brothers and nieces and nephews as neighbors.

The orange trees grew big and got old, but the fruit stayed sweet. Something tight developed between the Morgans and those orange trees, but, as happens, time brought troubles. Winters began turning cold. The orange trees froze and died, and the grove dwindled, tree by tree.

Raymond Morgan, a boy among the original Florida Morgans, elevated to be the reigning family patriarch, feared their total loss. Raymond had grown up to be an old-school craftsman, a builder, a man who could fix anything, a fellow with pride who insisted on doing everything right. He loved his adopted homeplace and its special old Florida setting. The family's sense of this land, bordering on a swampy prairie and rich with wildlife, needed the accent of those orange trees. Years earlier, while his wife was still living, Raymond the craftsman made his first preservation move. He constructed a 27-piece scaffold around the few remaining orange trees. When the weatherman warned freezes were coming, he and son Kenny would pull a giant tarpaulin across that scaffold to protect the trees from the cold.

"It was a lot of trouble," Kenny told me in 1995. He, his wife, and their two children now live next door to Raymond, within hollering distance. "Next morning, we'd have to pull it back off so they could get air."

Even so, even with all that care, time and the weather could not be held back. All but two of the beloved orange trees died. Raymond decided something else had to be done. He got some poles from a utility company, posted them around the circumference of the trees, and rigged up a plastic cover that more easily could be pulled across the whole thing. One man could handle it, if necessary. This time he left room for air at the bottom.

Raymond, in his 70s and still a proud craftsman, stood ready for the next rigors of time and winter. His oranges might be the most expensive in Florida, but that was not the issue. This was a family thing, a Morgan matter. He had done everything he could to preserve his family, his land and his orange trees. He believed the Morgans would be there a long time, and he hoped he and the orange trees would be there with them. As always, he had done his job right.

This was an old-fashioned Florida story, about love of family and place, without the hurrah and accompanying nonsense that structured organizations and big-time government often bring to the scene when they try to make political hay from this sort of thing. Raymond would have no part of any of that. He wanted no strangers with political agendas messing around his life and his land. Outsiders never fully understand. Let the world fly down I-75, a few miles west, in pursuit of whatever absurdity it wished, and never mind. Home and how you cared for it were what mattered, and Raymond knew about that.

Florida, like Raymond Morgan with his orange trees, must invent its own solutions. If necessity is the mother of this process, then love should be the first ingredient.

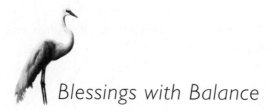

Blessings with Balance

Late one May or June morning, thunder growls, slowly getting its anger up. Winds, mostly southerly, begin herding the heat and moisture into mountainous clouds. Lightning cracks. In the afternoon, for an hour or two, rain bursts hard upon the Everglades. The South Florida rainy season begins.

After a winter of drying out and drowsing, the Everglades welcome the summer rains. Withered and scorched sawgrass livens and greens. Mudflats, which cracked and dried while the tourists were frolicking on the coasts, turn into nourishing ooze again. Turtles and frogs, and an immense variety of other life-forms ranging from tadpoles to alligators, take on renewed wriggle. The hot, wet rituals of summer rouse up the Glades.

Everything natural, except some people, welcomes summer in Florida. That too is natural. Between people and the rest of nature, there nearly always exists a contradiction or a conflict. The Everglades and South Florida's cities, like two small nations bumping borders, speak different languages and follow different customs. Their needs clash and threats arise.

In all seasons, the coexistence seems shaky, but in summer we notice the mutuality more easily. The shared need seems clearer. As summer stretches into six months of high noon, there is plenty of time to brood over it. Ninety degrees becomes par. Outside, we are heat-rich and comfort-poor.

In South Florida's cities, summer turns into a bittersweet time. City folk do not usually rejoice over the rains, however necessary they may be, even though the threat of flooding was removed from city streets years ago by canals and dikes, even though the rains drop sweetwater for the aquifers to absorb, and even though they also deliver a brief puff of cooler air and sometimes even freshening hail. Still, they routinely are greeted by more curses of annoyance than cheers of appreciation. They slicken asphalt and douse clothing and interrupt baseball games. They hinder more activities than they stimulate.

The cities need the rain to restock their supply of drinking water, but their migrated populations deplore the smothering heat and the constant wetness and the persistent mildew. Even well-acclimated natives struggle in the summer and regularly, along with the others, grumble as they dash from one air-conditioned cave to another.

The lowered Glades water levels in winter bother the turtles and alligators the way wet heat bothers the cities. A turtle, for example, digs into dried ponds until it finds moisture or mud, and there it enjoys lethargy, as long as the mud suits it, waiting for the reviving rain. Alligators do the same but with community result. In a drought, the last water in the Everglades usually can be found in an alligator den, for if necessary alligators can dig several feet down, all the way to bedrock, and find seeping water. They create an oasis for other animals in the process.

Summer plagues us and defines us. It dominates the nature of all Florida and all Floridians, but especially South Floridians. The landscape swells in beauty while we unfurl umbrellas and switch on paddle fans and and turn on air conditioners, like pacifiers, trying to induce calm. As the rains reach their peak and seem intolerably inconvenient and monotonous—in August and September (when, in some years, more than half of South Florida's average annual rainfall occurs)—we fight it by trying to remember the benefits.

Some Floridians, like migrating birds, take a summer break by fleeing to the mountains. Most, however, simply succumb to "the slows." In the absence of mud ponds, we close doors and windows and drapes and substitute air conditioners for mud. Then we sit back, lower our lids, and watch the world through plateglass windows, as though it were live TV.

Buzzards set a proper pace, circling with ease upon the thermal air currents above the cities. Tall palms stand like steamily troubled elders, fretful, first nodding yes and then shaking no. Biting bugs come to dinner, and you are it; in summer, Florida turns into a world capital for bugs.

Emotions come easy in the heat. We are brothers and sisters marinating in sweat, all of us clad in wet suits, all of us believers in shade. The sun puts soul into Florida as though it were steaming clams. Sweat is the proving essence. Frostproof and Winter Park and Sweetwater sweat, just as much as Devil's Garden and Boiling Creek and Roast Ear. Palm Beach sweats as much as Immokalee, and St. Petersburg as much as Steinhatchee. Heat frames the Florida idea, makes our rough edges droop. Tropical droop becomes the unofficial state posture.

The alligators get touchy and irritable, for they are in heat, too. It is mating season. Snakes crawl out of their holes and try to eat the pretty little eggs that the songbirds have laid on twig nests. The fish rise. The mosquitoes swarm. Poison ivy flourishes. Pollen takes flight. Sandspurs grow.

Officially, South Florida might be temperate zone, but the laws of the rain and the seasons are tropic, wrote Marjory Stoneman Douglas in *The Everglades: River of Grass*. These are laws that nobody breaks. Douglas defined the South Florida climate for us. She taught us that because of the Atlantic Ocean, the Gulf of Mexico, and the 700 square miles of Lake Okeechobee, we should consider south Florida a tropical island.

In summer, the trade winds (from the southeast) blow moist air upon the island steadily, day and night. The combination of conditions over the Glades amounts to a rain machine, contended the late Art Marshall, renowned conservationist and Everglades champion. So the rainfall patterns and totals follow tropic proportions, splashing the region unevenly but averaging 60 or so inches a year, most of it from those lightning-accented storms. (A slow-moving hurricane, though, can drop 30 to 40 inches of rain in 24 hours.)

The lightning is special. It rages across Lightning Alley, a middle portion of the peninsula renowned as the most active lightning region in the United States. Florida leads the nation in lightning deaths and the alley averages 100 thunderstorms per year between May and October. Blame extreme temperate shifts and the wind patterns of an ocean-influenced peninsula.

Sometimes, the summer mischief turns even more extreme. During the awful heat, hurricanes come howling across the ocean from the direction of Africa, and gambling time begins. Against the certain knowledge that from June to October giant whirlwinds will come raging out of the ocean toward land, Floridians—especially those living on the coasts and in high-rises standing at water's edge—bet that these one-eyed demons on the prowl will not stumble into the right Caribbean path or conditions and crash into their homes.

Hurricane Andrew, which hit south Florida on August 24, 1992, killing 38 (directly or indirectly), demolishing 25,000 homes and causing $20 billion in property damage (according to *The Miami Herald*), altered complacency and made the bet a more grim gamble. Suddenly, South Florida had at least a million new experts on the ferociousness of hurricanes, as well as persuasively personal accounts of their horrors. Hurricane Andrew caused one of the worst disasters ever in the United States, and hurricanes in general became real and present threats again.

Until then, the ranking teller of hurricane stories probably was Bernard Russell of Islamorada in the Florida Keys. I talked with Russell, a retired yacht captain, boatbuilder, and cabinetmaker, several times over the years about the hurricanes he had known, especially the monster in 1935 that had winds greater than 200 miles per hour and killed 408 persons, including 50 members of his family. He remembered it well.

Bernard was 17 then, but memories of that Labor Day night stayed fresh for him. "You can't visualize anything that awesome," he told me in 1992. "It was pure hell." His head had felt as though it would explode. The first surge of water pushed under the door of his home, and an 18-foot tide (plus waves breaking 10 feet higher) followed and squashed the house. In that storm, Bernard's mother, grandmother, sisters, aunts, uncles, cousins died. The storm surge tore one sister from Bernard's grasp, and he never saw her again. Railroad tracks were bent like hairpins. Railroad cars were thrown 400 feet off their tracks. Cars were hammered into the ground like nails. Only 11 members of the family were left. This was a family that had fled North Carolina after the American Revolution and settled in the Bahamas. They left the Bahamas in 1860 to homestead 162 acres in Islamorada (including Windley Key). The Russells were Conch royalty.

"We had to start life over again from scratch," Bernard said. "We had nothing." What he had was experience that taught him to hang on, to endure, to survive. His golden advice for Floridians who might forget history and discount hurricane realities: "Don't ever take one of those things lightly."

Dr. Neil Frank never did. Long before Hurricane Andrew made the message so clear, he went around the state every year like a scientific Chicken Little, warning that one day the sky would fall. He would show slide pictures of terrible destruction and explain how it happened and why. He would elaborate on the inevitability of hurricanes and the odds that one might happen this year.

Dr. Frank, then director of the Hurricane Center in Coral Gables, was a sincere prophet of doom and terror. Audiences loved him. It was a puzzlement, he explained to me once in 1985, before he retired to Texas as a televison forecaster.

In his public talks, he related the oddities and the quirks that mix into the tragedies of hurricanes—tales of death, which arrives on a giant wave during a hurricane party, and pictures showing only bare pilings left from "hurricane-proof" buildings. The audience nearly always found a place to laugh. Dr. Frank never laughed. Linking hurricanes to Florida's crowded coasts scared him.

Some doubted that hurricanes were the bogeymen that Dr. Frank claimed they were. They would walk away from his sermons, quoting from his nightmare scenarios and chuckling. Others would be ready to complain about the inconvenience of evacuation orders that came before it was certain a hurricane would arrive. Some would brag about living in a good, solid home and speculate about 'riding out' any storm than came.

Quietly, sincerely, Dr. Frank kept preaching. You have to understand, he would tell them, that nine out of 10 people who die in a hurricane are drowned by a storm surge—a dome of water maybe 50 miles wide that hits the coastline where the eye of the hurricane makes landfall. The coastal islands and beaches might go under 10 or 15 or even more feet of water. Waves would break against (and probably collapse) the second-or third-story walls of those buildings erected with solid enough and deep enough pilings still to be standing despite the scouring away of sand underneath them. Nobody, he pointed out, except the builder knew for sure which buildings had adequate pilings. Besides that, no building code then offered protection against storm surges. None, he said.

Dr. Frank would show a slide. "In a hurricane, the water rises enough that the waves knock in the front walls of these buildings, and then the wind takes the roof off. It is very common," he said.

Establishing that no one near the water can be certain of safety during a major hurricane, he continued. He cited studies that showed (in 1985) it would take about 21 hours to evacuate the southeast coast (Dade, Broward, Palm Beach counties), about 30 hours to evacuate the Florida Keys, 27 hours to evacuate the southwest coast from Sarasota down to Naples, 18 hours to evacuate the Tampa Bay area. He said that because of population growth, the evacuation time would increase one hour each year (10 years, for example, 10 additional hours for each region).

The problem was, he said, forecasters cannot guarantee enough warning time to allow for evacuation. He estimated that—24 hours in advance—the average forecasting error would be "roughly 115 miles" and noted that a hurricane's area of destruction was 75 to 100 miles wide. So the only safe decision 24 hours in advance would be to evacuate 100 miles on either side of the 100-mile probable area of landfall, or an area of 300 miles. "Two thirds to three fourths of the people who evacuate with 24-hour lead time are going to do so unnecessarily," he said. For emphasis, he put it another way. "For every four times we tell you to evacuate, only one will be necessary." Because evacuation is disruptive and expensive, and because three out of four times it proves to have been unnecessary, when long periods pass without a major hurricane striking Florida apathy grows.

"That bothers me," Dr. Frank said. "But that is the price we're going to have to pay if we continue to let people come on the coastline the way we have in the past."

Neil Frank, Dr. Chicken Little, warned there would be "meteorological surprises." Such a surprise, as he defined it, was when a weak hurricane close to the coast strengthened into a major hurricane during the final hours before landfall—too late for an evacuation warning. He cited the Labor Day 1935 hurricane in the Keys (the one that cost the Bernard Russell family so dearly). In that one, a disturbance only strong enough to be called a tropical storm left Andros Island in the Bahamas and 30 hours later hit the Florida Keys with winds higher than 200 miles per hour. The question thus arose: since it takes 30 hours to evacuate the Keys, does that mean they should be evacuated every time there is a tropical storm in the Bahamas?

"I don't know the answer, folks," Dr. Frank said.

Dr. Frank called it a puzzle of human behavior. He was being kind. It's crazy.

As a matter of pride, Floridians can strain at their calendars and build a case that they have all the traditional seasons—not only summer, but fall, winter and spring, too—but the case is shaky.

Summer in South Florida by temperature begins in late March and lasts until October or November. In North Florida, it begins in May and lasts until September.

In South Florida, the brief fall could occur during the playing of the national anthem before a University of Miami football game. In North Florida, it begins in October with cool nights and fades toward winter when the migrating sandhill cranes arrive about Thanksgiving. Fall announces itself in the upper peninsula when a cool northwester drives the mullet into shallow water around Cedar Key. It begins open confession in the Panhandle when the dogwoods and sweetgums take on splashes of red and yellow and when the oysters get fat in Apalachicola, a special time.

Usually by late October the breeze blows across Apalachicola Bay lightly burdened by chill as well as the usual whiff of eau de mullet. Men stand in the bows of long, low boats and scratch the bottom of the bay with oyster tongs. Pickup trucks line U.S. 98 along the weatherbeaten seafood houses of East Point, and the piles of oyster shells being tossed out on the bank grow like hedges.

Fall is the best time of the year in Apalachicola, a bump on the underbelly of the Panhandle where the Apalachicola River—deliciously saturated with Alabama and Georgia mud—gushes its sweet water into the salinity of a Gulf bay guarded by barrier islands. In the days before the horrors of pollution crippled the bay, and when it had time to recover from occasional hurricane trauma, the bay produced 85 percent of Florida's oysters.

"The Apalachicola Bay oyster has a better taste than any other oyster in the world," George Kirvin told me in 1978. He was a native Floridian, owned a major seafood house and was a man of stature in Apalachicola. "It's a known fact that an oyster will grow faster in this bay than anywhere else in the world," he said. Despite being known as the Gentleman Fisherman, he appeared ready to gaff you in the nearest thing you had to a gill if you disagreed. I did not disagree then, nor in the many other trips made to Apalachicola in later years to verify his wisdom.

Most winters, south Florida has none, not that a Snowbird would recognize, anyway. When there is one, it might happen on a Tuesday or a Wednesday in February. The flowers bloom and the sun shines and vegetables grow beautifully in the mucklands around Okeechobee and the farmlands around Homestead, south of Miami. The rare freeze becomes a disaster.

Fold the Florida map horizontally in the middle. Just about where the wrinkle falls, probably around Haines City or maybe as low as Lake Wales, there lies the mythical frost line, Florida's version of an equator. Below it, true cold is not usual, but that depends on those variable human thermostats. In a six-hour winter's drive from Melrose to Miami, the world can change from cold and quaintly Cracker to warm and cosmopolitan. With temperatures in the 50s, North Florida newspapers pronounce the weather cool and nice; at the same temperatures in South Florida, the papers call it chilly. North Florida suffers winters that for the most part would seem like spring in Minnesota. Still, it has frost frequently, and sometimes ice (rarely, snow). Cold snaps last a few days at a stretch anytime between early December and March, sometimes as late as Easter. The Panhandle in winter, though, is a different place with its own special character and personality.

For someone weary of the lockstep life, the Panhandle in winter has the comfortable reality of Grandma's country home: lots of charm, totally real, maybe a bit inconvenient. The likelihood of seeing an old-fashioned Floridian in his original habitat increases at the same time that the flavors and sounds of Alabama and Georgia grow more prominent. It could be as real as a surprise embrace or a bruise on the nose.

After each visit, you came away feeling you were somewhere that represents an authentic native dimension in the state. The scenes of the highlands, along the 200 miles that the Panhandle stretches from Tallahassee to Pensacola, stayed with you—stark, vital, beautiful in their own way, not really defined and captured yet by any artist, but powerful and ripe and waiting for one to come along. Early on cold mornings, steam would rise from roadside ditches and fog would cloak the pastures. The roads trailed across real hills, the most distinctive ones that Florida has, and naked trees stood above fields made picturesque by the short stubble of hay or by plowed furrows laid bare and bloodless like old wounds.

As you traveled U.S. 90 between Crestview and Chipley, you could not fail to notice the big-sky effect, the patterns of clouds that suggested significance and encouraged study. Monuments to past life marked the landscape: old frame houses with rusting tin roofs squatting lonesomely on hills, fragrant wood smoke spiraling from chimneys distinguished by faded bricks and chipped mortar, evergreen pines rising straight and disciplined above scrawny scrub oaks with rust-scarlet leaves.

Hunters' pickup trucks parked along the highways, hunters leaning on their guns nearby, smoking, drinking, their companions off in the brush. In the back of some of the trucks there were the bloody carcasses of deer.

There was a feeling that the battles of life were being fought on open ground, won and lost and continually rejoined. There was a sense of traditional life, of hard times that became good memories, of family tragedies and joys that put benchmarks in lives. The churches and the cemeteries and schools suggested that chains of generations did not easily break. In the cafés, old-timers compared temperatures and ice sightings and drank a lot of coffee while talking about Alabama and Florida State University football.

Winter freezes turned those highland hills into subdued brown and gold, with minor shades of red and yellow and green, tourists were few, and the natives relaxed. Settlers from South Florida and elsewhere came to the upper Panhandle looking for a way of life, lost earthiness, and a sense of community no longer available in cities.

The Panhandle had an upstairs and a downstairs, and Grandma's country home was the upstairs, the rural side of the Panhandle. The downstairs was the beautiful Gulf Coast, tourist Florida, from Mexico Beach west to Pensacola Beach, the area that lured most visitors and commerce, gradually transfusing it with new blood and character. The beaches in winter were too cool for swimming but better than ever for walking. There was a true off-season, and the crowds were slim. Between freezes, many middays were warm with evenings that brought a cool, attractive edge.

In winter, the Panhandle put on no airs. You got it straight. Reality was the thing. It reminded you that theories and plans and progress did not bleed, but humans did.

Spring in South Florida might occur between 5 P.M. and sunset anytime during March or April. In North Florida, in the good years, especially in the interior, spring might fill April with a sweetness not usually associated with Florida.

During March, you could catch those fleeting spring hours as you approached Fort Pierce from the west through the cow prairies and the orange groves. Driving across those broad sweeps of flat pasture, broken in the distance only by island-clumps of pines and palms, there was the faint, rich aroma of cow manure. As the late afternoon sun slanted across those islands, the browns and greens of the trees first glowed a bit gold and then soft pink, nicely accented by heavy shadows. These were the scenes so loved and so brilliantly captured by the artist Beanie Backus of Fort Pierce. Out of his head and heart and down through his fingertips there came inspiration that preserved these cow prairies and tree islands and pine forests forever on canvas. The miles passed, and you moved past the prairies and into blossoming orange groves, laid across the land like a canopy. The heavy, sweet perfume of the blossoms induced a natural high, and you entered Fort Pierce with a smile.

Putting all that—plus the seasonal shadings that occur in Central Florida and the Panhandle—into the strictures of a calendar becomes clumsy, if not stupid. Florida has its own seasons, a lot of them. The basic ones are Hot and Cool, plus Wet and Dry. There also is Snowbird Season. It usually includes In-Law Season, which requires stocking the refrigerator with extra food and drink and learning how to smile while thoroughly dismayed. The pain comes in crimped pocketbooks and small-talk paralysis. There also is Mosquito Season, Lovebug Season, Hurricane Season, Sinkhole Season (when droughts fluctuate levels of the water table, and weakened underground limestone caverns collapse). On the plus side there are Oyster Season and Stonecrab Season and Mullet Season and a string of others like that.

Exposure to Florida's seasonal peculiarities changes you. Not many who move to Florida fully understand in advance what happens. Among other things, it can be hazardous to a Snowbird's thermostat.

Most newcomers understand the informality of customs and clothing, and that in this land of the youthfully ancient a different sense of time prevails. Some also appreciate that the subtlety of Florida's seasons represents a unique enhancement in the nature cycle. Some sense the rich social orchestration offered by Florida's varied languages and accents.

Fewer grasp and endorse the growing Florida idea that it can be danger-ous to spray pesky mosquitoes because the spray also poisons the bugs that birds eat. Rare are those who arrive wise to the fact that smelly swamps or wetlands represent assets rather than nuisances to be bull-dozed clean, or that our pastel and bleached-bone colors do not identify exotics but are simply strong defenses against the sun. Almost none, how-ever, adopts Florida with proper anticipation of what life here will do to personal thermostats.

In Florida, the body in time tends to lose its ability to distinguish be-tween what should be considered warm and cool, at least in terms of na-tional standards of temperature measurements. In other words, the ther-mostat fails. A South Floridian can see a reading of 42 or even 52 degrees and label it a freezing temperature. Or, it can be 80 and cool, or 80 and warm, or 80 and just right.

The common explanation is that continual exposure to upper range temperatures thins the blood. Whether it is an actual thinning of the blood, or merely psychological conditioning, is debatable. On observed evidence, I tend to believe in conditioning.

I know a Floridian whose wife fiddled so much with the thermostat in their house, precipitating with each change of the season a battle to estab-lish at what ideal parallel the mercury line should rest, that he finally gave her a thermostat all her own. What he did not explain was that her private thermostat was not hooked up. He maintained a secret thermostat that controlled the actual temperature. When she became uncomfortable with the temperature, she had free rein to run her thermostat up and down all day if she wished, according to her passing moods of heat or chill. It did not change anything, but she thought it did, and this made her perfectly happy—a typical case of the Florida thermostat.

In Florida, comfort eventually succumbs to influences that reduce de-pendence on the actual temperature. The fabled humidity is a factor, but not the only one. As the thermostat begins to malfunction, the weather becomes a matter of interpretation. New Floridians in this beguilingly informal setting quickly begin to harmonize with higher temperature ranges. They adjust their defenses. They learn to expect sunshine and breezes almost every day, as though guaranteed. They learn to shuck off all but the essential clothing. They become accustomed to having the bright, inviting outdoors always available.

Nothing is so easy to get used to as luxury, and most Florida weather is a luxury (though some might argue about August). The Floridian becomes conditioned to high expectations. When temperatures are marginally cool, a passing cloud suggests chill. When there is a marginal chill, the Floridian complains of freezing. If it really freezes, he feels a sense of tragedy. When the breezes blow as guaranteed, the heat and the humidity are bearable problems. Only if it becomes still, and the air seems to disappear, does he complain. Eventually, the new Floridian adapts. He comes down with the Florida ailment—thermostat atrophy. Forever after, he will be a maverick about temperatures.

¶ Migration figures confirm there is broad understanding in the land that not living in Florida can be hazardous to your health. As many as a thousand such believers might move into the state on any single day. Less clear are the risks.

For example, when a freeze envelops Florida, it is more than just a change in the weather, much more. Freeze disorients people who believe that ice belongs in a glass, not all over the community. Goose bumps spoil a tan. Heavy coats smother a sunshine spirit. Chapped lips cannot whistle the true Florida tune.

A freeze invades like a rogue enemy out of control. Briefly, Florida seems like a conquered land. Our way of life suffers an alien plague. We are prisoners of a sort. Consider these diary notes recorded on a freezing North Florida day in 1986:

> Maybe the wind has calmed and the sun shines brightly for you now, friend. Maybe you are sweating. Maybe the windows are open again, and the freeze is over. But on the day that I write this, we are under siege from winter. To understand your blessings, remember it with me.
>
> The day beams sharp and clear, but the cold is bone-deep. The sun has no power. It merely makes the frost glow. The thermometer confesses to 20 degrees, and the thin red line keeps dropping. The windows frost. Snow flurries have been reported. The wind howls in attack. Limbs break off the trees. The power flickers, threatening blackout.
>
> Every few minutes, between air-conditioning commercials, radio bulletins detail a severe freeze warning and advise that we take proper precau-

tions. It is a little like hearing that the Russians are coming, that they are at the county line and moving fast, ignoring the 55-mph law, and the heaviest weapon we have on hand is bug spray.

The radio adds the small comfort that the invasion will not last long. We can expect to be dead only for about three days, it suggests. Never mind the freeze-calluses you may have developed in New York or Ohio or some other foreign place. Forget that. This is different. Florida houses are not meant to be igloos.

For Florida, a severe freeze is scary, super-unnatural stuff. It kills things not supposed to die seasonally and cripples a lot of others. Florida nurtures warm life only. Neither we nor our landscape have real defenses against severe cold, and always remember that local definition determines severe cold.

The temperature does not have to dive down to zero or something bizarre like that. Anything below freezing qualifies as severe. Whatever freezes an orange will freeze a Floridian, too. Some, mostly native South Floridians, suffer even more easily. To them, anything cool enough to create a shiver is Eskimo stuff, an arctic wave. They shiver if the temperature does not stay above the retirement age. No matter what you have heard, among Florida families blood is not thicker than water.

On this memorable, frigid day at my home in North Central Florida, we try to survive by stacking up oak logs in the fireplace and digging out the warm clothes, most of them old ones, and dreaming about better days. We are moved to wonder what malign force has begun to distort fair Florida. Winter should be only a dash of sparkle for our temperate and subtropical delights. For the third time in four winters, the weather has turned rude, uncouth. Severe cold should be an exception and surprise, not a habit.

Whatever happened to the warm Florida winters of my childhood? Has my memory gone bad, or has the weather run amok?

Pretty folk never freeze, the Crackers say, and that is the way it should be. All Floridians believe they have pretty souls at least, but in recent winters the inner beauty has been disguised by red faces and runny noses.

We stay isolated in our house, or better yet in our warm beds, and peer out the fogged windows at the havoc. The birds are not singing. The squirrels dig in the ground, searching for lost caches of acorns. Withered brown leaves blow across the yard, making scratching sounds, as though the earth itself needs to satisfy a strange itch.

The newspaper tries to comfort us with harrowing reports from the real north. They regale us with ice storms and blizzards. They imply the truth of comparative misfortune, but it does not penetrate personal discomfort.

A severe freeze in Florida is a peculiar time. It registers in coordination with the thermometer. The lower it dips into Florida, the odder the experience. It is worth cataloguing like this while the details are fresh, that it may be puzzled over in August.

So I write this during these icy days, and I tap it into the computer. My mood is that of a man on a remote island, slipping a message into a bottle and tossing it out into the sea. I calculate that it will bob up eventually.

The world ought to know, ought to understand, what it is like when severe freeze marches down the peninsula, laying waste to citrus trees and pretty flowers and sweet illusions. As Sherman said about war, this is hell. Perhaps even worse. Hell is warm.

So it goes. Florida weather is not like any other, no matter how it seems to outsiders. Each season has its own blessings and surprises.

History at a Fantastic Trot

The arrivals of strangers tell the Florida story. Decade after decade, wave after wave, chapter after chapter, they washed over the state as repetitiously as tides. Even historic cities such as Pensacola, Fernandina Beach, St. Augustine, and Key West, whose stories anchored at principal historic starting points, had fresh beginning after beginning as new people and new ideas arrived, becoming ascendant in imaginative ways. The tales of how that happened are individual and many. Some of the lesser known ones turned out to be the most fascinating to me.

In less easily accessible places, especially in the interior, Florida developed late and came on fast—at a trot, if not a gallop. Okeechobee—perched at the top of the great lake covering 730 square miles in the heart of South Florida—experienced that. The telescoping of development there suggested the pace of history in Florida.

The Raulersons were the first non-Indian family to settle in Okeechobee. In three generations, or one man's lifetime, the Okeechobee area went from naturally wild country inhabited by Indians to a frontier and finally to the Florida of real-estate salesmen and subdivisions.

The Raulersons were there every step of the way. As railroads and electricity and telephones and paved roads came in, they evolved from pioneer cattlemen to merchants, bankers, churchmen, and city fathers. Their story is a true Florida sample.

The first Raulerson was Noel, who came to Florida from south Georgia and settled in Polk County, meeting and marrying Tempa Whidden. There in 1857 their first son, Peter, was born. He would have six brothers and sisters. In 1874, looking for more land and fewer people, Noel Raulerson trailed his cattle, numbering in the thousands, south across country to Fort Basinger on the Kissimmee River north of Lake Okeechobee, and made that home.

In Basinger, Peter met Louisiana Chandler, so named because she was the first child born after her family arrived in Florida aboard a sailing sloop from Louisiana. They married and began a second generation of Raulersons native to Florida. From Basinger, the Raulersons could drive their cattle across state to Punta Rassa (near what is now Sanibel Island) on the west coast for shipping to Cuba and other places.

In 1895 Peter, restless and looking for the right place just as his father had, moved east to the Bend, a place between the Kissimmee River and Taylor Creek, which in time would become the city of Okeechobee. He was the first white settler, four years ahead of the next one. There, he homesteaded 160 acres, built his family a two-story log house. He hauled his family from Basinger on a cart pulled by three yokes of oxen across the watery flats to their new home. He stayed in Okeechobee until his death in 1947, a lifetime that stretched from frontier to city.

Hiram Raulerson, Peter's grandson, ran a store in Okeechobee. During the 1970s I visited him and his delightful wife, Annie, several times. At our first meeting, on Shrove Tuesday, they fed me pancakes at the Episcopal church, and over the years they introduced me to the history of Okeechobee. In the process, I learned about the history of the Raulersons.

Hiram, born in 1903, a genteel grandfather of 10 who wore a tie even in 90-degree heat, sometimes would find time to talk between tending customers at his men's store. Because of his family he understood Okeechobee as few others could. For him, it had a personal dimension. He had sampled the American experience in miniature.

Hiram, for example, attended a one-room schoolhouse (founded by his family) where a single teacher taught eight grades. Indians traded at his father's store, the first in Okeechobee. He had cowboys in the family; they came with the cattle business. He remembered when cows and hogs roved the streets freely, and when catfishermen and cowboys fought in public with knives, fists, and guns.

Commercial fishing began on Lake Okeechobee about 1900. Most of it was by haul seine and the catch was shipped on dredged-out water routes to Fort Myers, Kissimmee, and Fort Lauderdale. When the railroad reached Okeechobee in 1915—providing quicker transportation out— catfishing jumped to an annual gross of one million dollars. Iced barrels of catfish were loaded on railroad cars and shipped north at the rate of up to 10 cars a week. In 1924 an estimated 6.5 million pounds of catfish were shipped from the lake. In 1925, with sportsfishermen claiming the lake was being ruined, a state law declared all seining in freshwater illegal; the fishermen countered by having Lake Okeechobee declared "not fresh water." It was a dispute that would continue.

U.S. Senator Duncan Fletcher (D., Fla.) revealed a possible reason for the rise in catfish popularity when he testified in 1929 at congressional hearings that as the catfish reached northern markets it turned into salmon. Others said a catfish filet magically changed to filet of sole when it went north.

¶ On weekends, the cowboys from the ranches north of the lake would gather "uptown" and the catfishermen off the lake would gather "downtown" around Taylor Creek. Inevitably, moonshine and blood flowed. Old-timer R. M. Dupree, probably the oldest catfisherman on the lake at the time I talked with him in in 1979, remembered those times well: "They were both rough. Yessir. You might not believe this, but I've seen as many as 15 fights going on at one time. Fishermen and them cowhunters. They'd just gather up. They'd get to drinking, and you'd hear one holler after a while, and then they'd all get to hollering, and first thing you know they'd meet up and go at it. Once they got to drinking that moonshine, they'd just fight for the fun of it." One catfisherman, according to Dupree, loved to get a shoeshine every Saturday night—it somehow nursed his ego—but when the fighting started, he would lose the shoes. He solved the problem by getting his bare feet shined.

Hiram Raulerson had his own memories of all that. He told the story of how his pioneering grandfather, Peter, also Okeechobee's first mayor, dealt with outlaw gangs and carousing catfishermen who routed local law enforcement. Gentle folk stayed off the streets on weekend nights. In those days, when a deputy sheriff was sent over from Fort Pierce to bring order, local rowdies would meet him at the bridge and throw him in the river. Mayor Peter Raulerson countered by appointing the toughest cat-fisherman he could find—a man called Pogy Bill Collins—as policeman. After that, the gangs tread softly and the cowboys and fishermen began to recognize higher authority. Pogy Bill later won election as sheriff and became a legendary figure of checkered reputation.

Hiram witnessed the steamboat days (goods from upstate delivered via steamboats on the Kissimmee River). He saw the great cattle drives across state to Punta Rassa, the coming of Flagler's railroad (1915) and his Model Land Company, which laid out the town grid, the paving of highways (1924), the arrival of magical electric lights and the conveniences of piped water, the diking of Lake Okeechobee, which converted marshes into pastures. Peter and Louisiana started the first post office (an Octagon soapbox under Peter's bed, according to area historian Lawrence Will). As a county commissioner, Peter rode a horse 36 miles to Fort Pierce to attend commission meetings. A local hospital was named for Louisiana.

Hiram's father, Lewis, who opened the first store, also opened the first bank. Hiram saw Okeechobee blossom into a city that dreamed of being "another Chicago" (because it, too, was on a great lake). He lived through monster hurricanes (1926 and 1928). He married Annie the day before his father's bank failed in the Great Depression. If hard times temporarily shrank dreams to gratitude just for survival, the Raulersons managed to come back strong. Annie served the community through the Red Cross, the church, the historical society, and a variety of clubs. She received the first key to the city ever given an Okeechobee citizen. Hiram took over the store, following his father, and became a county commissioner, as his grandfather had.

From 1895 to 1950, the Okeechobee area went from almost no population to about 3,500 in the county. By 1978, when Hiram toted it up, there were some 22,000 people, most of them centered around the city, and growing fast. Tourists and fishermen raised those numbers each winter. After years of isolation from the growth that layered development along Florida's coasts, Okeechobee joined the crowd. A look of newness began to sweep over the town, a scene far different from beginnings just 83 years earlier.

"Grandfather was a remarkable man," Hiram said. "About six feet tall. Had gray, curly hair. He rode horses until he was well past 80. Grandmother was short. Their house was the unofficial community center. Everybody went there, and she cooked huge meals. Even for breakfast they had two kinds of meat, and biscuits. He had his own ways. He liked to take a toddy [water and sugar and moonshine] two or three times a day, but he never abused it. He would take one before breakfast, maybe one in the middle of the day, and then one again at night when he came in tired.

"The family was the center of life in those days. They played the fiddle and the piano and sang and square-danced and made syrup and candy. It was different. We would think of it as a hardship now, but they didn't think so."

Hiram could look out his store window and see the past, present, and probable future of Okeechobee. He saw it all as a historical chain, from his grandfather Peter to his father, Lewis, and then to him and his grandchildren. That was their Florida out there.

New arrivals in Florida came pursuing dreams of all sorts, but the lure of land and accompanying get-rich spiels ran high among them. J. T. Casebourne found out about that as a British lad of 22 who considered himself worldly wise from experience on a rubber plantation in Singapore and from World War I duty with the Royal Field Artillery. In 1911, he met a man in Liverpool who was selling just such dreams.

The man pitched a new town created just for small farmers, in tropical South Florida, where the soil was so incredibly rich that vegetables would jump out of the ground and grow fat and tall. The fellow handed out brochures that pictured luscious, red-ripe tomatoes. These were enough to sway young Casebourne's caution. "Mother staked me to $1,000 and said that was it. I could go to Florida if I liked," he told me in 1976, more than a half century after the adventure.

Casebourne pursued the dream and went, but with foresight decided not to buy the land just yet. He took an option on 10 acres. With the papers in his pocket Casebourne crossed the Atlantic, caught a train down to Palm Beach, and at the depot met a man named H. G. Geer, who was driving a Cadillac convertible. After a few days of seeing the sights, during which the tall, softly accented Britisher declined repeated offers to exercise the option before he saw the land, they piled into an overland touring car and headed west on what is now U.S. 441 toward the town of Geerworth.

About 25 miles out, they came to a canal that had no bridge over it. They drove the car upon a raft, used a chain to pull the raft across the canal, and forged on. "From there," as Casebourne remembered the story, "it was all muck land and a lot of water. We put the car in low gear and hoped." After another 13 miles, and an unestimated number of hours, they arrived.

Geerworth turned out to be a two-story frame hotel that sat without cheer on the broad Everglades plain. The hotel had a grocery store on the first floor. Six-foot-high partitions separated the bedrooms on the second. There also were a water tower and a few bungalows housing English and Scottish families.

"Somebody had planted tomatoes," Casebourne recalled. "The plants were enormously tall and green—but they wouldn't grow tomatoes. Nobody knew what to do." This was before soil scientists had discovered that certain soil additives could turn those mucklands into a winter vegetable kingdom. Casebourne worked as a carpenter and a boatman for a while and then left in September—a couple of years before the Florida land boom hit in a big way. Left behind were bitterness, confusion, and finally only a ghost town. The hurricane of 1926 wiped even that away.

From Geerworth, Casebourne went to Indianapolis, built a successful business, and, still remembering the old dream, retired to Florida in 1960. This time he chose Naples on the southwest Gulf Coast, winters only. Things had changed. His advice: never underestimate the power of the Florida dream. He bought it in Liverpool and never lost it, despite that mosquito-darkened, uncomfortable summer of 1922. He still wanted those mild winters and big, fat tomatoes.

Another newcomer, George S. Jennings, started his Florida experience with equally poor luck, an old-timer in North Florida told me. Jennings had an accident but made the most of it, and had a town named for him—Jennings, just two miles south of the Georgia boundary line, on U.S. 41.

The Jennings family, numbering six in all, left North Carolina in 1844 and cut overland across Georgia toward Florida. When they reached the Alapaha River, George S. Jennings built a raft and piled all their belongings on it, and then they climbed aboard and began floating south.

Near a high bluff just after they crossed into Florida, the river plunged into a pool, the Jennings family with it, and the raft never came out. Local stories varied from there. One said not enough water flowed out of the pool for the Jennings to continue. Another said the raft spun into a whirlpool, wrecked, and the Jennings family escaped with only a buttermilk churn.

Whatever, practical-minded George Jennings decided to settle there. The spot became known as Jennings' Defeat and the town that grew up nearby as Jennings. Afterward, Jennings discovered that the river reappeared in full force a mile or two downstream.

"Not much around Jennings anymore," said Roy Devane, an elderly Baptist preacher, in 1976. "But 40 or 50 years ago we had four cotton gins, two banks, and 15 or 20 stores. Boll weevil hit us hard back in the 'teens and changed things."

For years, Jennings' Defeat was Roy Devane's favorite fishing hole. He quit going there because too many people found out about it. Fishing and thinking, he said, are better done alone.

Devane had seen Jennings rise and fall with cotton, truck farming, the Depression, tobacco, corn, and the coming and going of industry nearby. The first 40 years of his life he farmed. Then he ran a grocery store, became a preacher, helped carry the mail, and for six years drove a school bus. He was sitting on his front porch watching the traffic when I found him. The center of Jennings had become a convenience store, the post office, a service station, and the school. He spent his time preaching, tending his cats, visiting his wife in a nursing home, and watching Jennings grapple with life.

Devane took me out to see the Jennings graves at Jennings' Defeat. He rubbed a time-darkened stone with Spanish moss, and the legend appeared, showing that Jennings had been born in England in 1790 and had died in Jennings, Hamilton County, in 1860, buried next to his "consort," Eliza.

Preacher Devane studied those old stones a long time, as though a sermon had occurred to him. "Jennings," he finally said, "is one of these small towns where nobody can get away with anything so easy. We're all right here together, sort of in one lump. Some people don't like that. No, they sure don't. But for folks not trying to get away with anything, it makes it nice."

The Florida story spins out most entertainingly in those individual lives, in tale after tale of dreamers and seekers who left somewhere else and came to Florida with a vision of something better. Over the years, family after family gave me personal histories that included such accidental beginnings as driving a Model T to Florida and having it break down somewhere short of their chosen destination. The family then accepted fate and just settled where the car stopped. The sum of those lives and random choices shaped Florida. The state tends to take on the dynamic nature of the ingredients that physically formed it: sand and water spread over a submerged crust of native limestone croppings: new residents as sand, tourists as water, Crackers (or Florida natives) as the limestone crust.

Change was the distinguishing heartbeat. History had an arrythmic pulse. Roots flattened into the thin Florida soil less like anchors than feelers or antennae, as though to detect the next pressure or movement.

The population pump never stopped. From 1845, with statehood, for the next 150 years Florida grew at the rate of 10 new residents per hour. In some decades, the pace reached three times that. In any given year since World War II, Florida had millions of residents (as many as three million) who had lived in the state less than five years—more than an ample supply of fresh, innocent ignorance about the state's distinctions for the unscrupulous to exploit in the marketplace or at any election.

In 1845 Florida, a slave-state with fresh memories of Indian wars, had some 70,000 citizens (nearly nine times more than in 1821, when it became a U.S. territory). In the 1990s, as perhaps the most ethnically diverse state, it reached 14 million.

Steamboats gave way to railroads and airplanes, oyster-shell and two-rut roads made room for interstates. Dr. John Gorrie's invention of an ice-making machine in 1848 at Apalachicola led to air-conditioning, a partial taming of Florida heat that began to cool commercial houses in the 1920s. Radio and television spread the news in newly popular ways.

The great god real estate sold land by the sections, then by the acres, then by the feet. Some said agents sold swampland by the gallon. Running out of linear measurements, they turned to divisions of the buildings and of time itself—from selling single homes in perpetuity to selling condos in the 1950s and eventually to time-shares, which sold ownership by the weeks.

The numbers can be calculated easier than the human changes they brought. In terms of environment and physical beauty consumed, in terms of uprooting lives, in terms of elbow room and breathing space, in terms of creating a transient atmosphere that diffused civic responsibility, in terms of erasing familiar geographic peculiarities and distinctive cultural heritage, in terms of warping comfortable values and behavior the impact of this eternal transience and perpetual change were beyond measure.

Residents in Florida tended to feel more a sense of ownership in the state than a sense of kinship or belonging. The state became more a place of frolic and speculation than one of nurturing and preservation. More Floridians saw it in terms of financial options than in love of place. Home frequently was an investment, not a family shrine. Too many people cared less than they should have about building quality into their lives and their enterprises. Uncertainty did that. Hints of these things came in other numbers from the University of Florida, showing Florida ranking high among the major states in the statistics of stress: in divorce, suicide, crime, the death rate, and the rate of fatal motor vehicle accidents.

When you put it all together, Florida emerged as a state without orthodoxy, a condition that created opportunity as well as risk. It became everyman's land, and thus no-man's-land, where eclectic philosophies and flavors and appetites remained distinct and apart. Reality at any moment could be hard to define, but the state remained perpetually expectant, forgetful of the past, always awaiting the next tide and betting that tomorrow would save today.

In St. Augustine, behind a stone wall and an iron gate that nudge up close to narrow Charlotte St., inside a vaultlike building opening on a courtyard, resides the St. Augustine Historical Society (SAHS), the historical conscience of the nation's oldest city. Scholars reasonably can argue that the St. Augustine Historical Society significantly affects the historical conscience of all Florida, even the nation.

Inside thick walls, the society's library has the invitingly cool and cloistered ambience of a Spanish wine cellar. There are little wooden tables worn smooth by patient scholars, stacks of books and papers and maps and photostats of documents dating to 1594. Genealogists flock there to study family histories.

The society originally formed in 1883 as the St. Augustine Institute of Science and has been busy and challenged ever since because of its reversing view of a city's usual problems: members as a group worried less about things becoming old than about things becoming new.

The society's first project was to save Fort Matanzas, 14 miles south of St. Augustine, on the Matanzas Inlet. The inlet, whose Spanish name means *place of slaughter,* commemorated the spot where Spanish forces in 1565 killed some 200 Frenchmen after capturing them in battle. In 1569, the Spanish put a wooden watchtower on the inlet and nearly 200 years later, in 1742, erected a stone tower there in the style of a Moorish fort. Because that fort was threatened with destruction, the society addressed an appeal to the secretary of war, and Fort Matanzas became a national monument.

The St. Augustine preservation idea preceded the SAHS, however. It probably had formal birth in 1856, when state leaders met upstairs at a St. George Street store owned by George Burt to discuss how they might save the city and its relics. Out of that meeeting came the Florida Historical Society.

The St. Augustine Historical Society first operated out of the Alcázar Hotel, one of Henry Flagler's creations, and other temporary housing until the war department licensed it as official custodian of the old riverfront Spanish fort, the Castillo de San Marcos, an arrangement that continued 20 years (until 1935, when the National Park Service took over). In 1918 it identified the structure at 14 St. Francis Street as the Oldest House, bought it, and turned it into a museum house open to tourists. That began an ambitious program of acquiring and rehabilitating historic sites or buildings, some of which were later resold with restrictive deed covenants in an attempt to assure their preservation. The society fought for history wherever it was threatened, whether in the maintenance of old cemeteries or against the federal four-laning of the highway along the bayfront near the Castillo (a battle lost, in 1947).

In time, it became apparent that the size of the challenges was becoming so large that it needed organized help, from the government, if possible. That realization, an idea which had been discussed since the 1930s, resulted in the state's creation of the Historic St. Augustine Preservation

Board, a state agency that in turn created the San Agustin Antiguo district and became the principal historic entity in the city. The society, however, remained an important force through its publications, the Oldest House museum store, and its library resources.

So history dominated is St. Augustine and so prestigious the society that once a call with a noise complaint was directed to the society library. The volunteer librarian politely explained that noise violations still remained police business.

Threats to historic St. Augustine usually came from pseudohistory in ticky-tacky, contrived tourist trappings that clustered around the legitimate realities and tended to stain their truths, but sometimes the threat simply was the pressure of tourism and population growth. In 1875, there was a proposal to tear down the Castillo itself to make room for a new railway terminal. In 1886, so many tourists were chipping souvenirs off the walls and sentry-boxes that public fears were raised that the Castillo would simply disappear. In 1907 there was a local movement to tear down the old stone gate at the northern entrance to historic St. George Street in favor of something more attractive. In the 1990s, the overburdens of traffic forced the revival of considerations to replace the Bridge of Lions across the Matanzas River, a landmark erected in 1927 with marble lion embellishments commissioned by a prominent local citizen to remedy St. Augustine's lack of Italian sculpture.

From the crest of that bridge a visitor could see the most history-loaded view in all of Florida. Looking toward town, the Castillo de San Marcos was on the right, and directly ahead and to the left was the old town fronted by a Spanish plaza. The view included narrow streets, old buildings, the 1793 Basilica Cathedral, plus late-19th-century hotels built by pioneer Henry Flagler that eventually were turned into government buildings and Flagler College.

❡ All of that had its beginning 55 years before the Puritans landed at Plymouth Rock, 42 years before the creation of historic Jamestown, Virginia. The Spaniard Don Pedro Menéndez de Avilés founded St. Augustine in 1565. He resolved to Christianize the Indians and create a civilized European colony, beginning the erasure of a Native American civilization that had existed for thousands of years. Spanish rule of St. Augustine lasted (though interrupted) for 235 years. Not until the year 2056 will the U.S. tenure be able to match that.

During their first century in St. Augustine, the Spanish built nine wooden forts, one after the other. In 1672, on orders from Queen Mariana, construction started on a more permanent one, the Castillo de San Marcos. Luis Rafael Arana, a National Parks historian who had studied the Castillo for more than a quarter century, provided perspective when I talked with him in 1981. This fort would be made of coquina (shellstone) mined from nearby Anastasia Island and from tabby (a fabrication of that shellstone) and would be erected in the sand along Matanzas Bay to protect the city. Thirty-one of the next 100 years were devoted to the building of that Castillo, Arana said.

At their base, the completed fort's stone walls were 13 feet thick; at the top, nine feet. When enemies laid siege to it, cannonballs penetrated but were held in the coquina walls. Arana said an exasperated attacker once described it as like "sticking a knife into cheese."

The Spanish quarreled with or fought the British, French, and the emerging United States, but the fort was never taken in battle. Three times, control changed hands by treaty (Spanish to British in 1763, British to Spanish in 1784, Spanish to U.S. in 1821), causing sudden and significant population turnovers. Left behind after all that was an international mélange of history with dominant Hispanic strains, including the Castillo, the most important historical structure in Florida and the most important Hispanic historical structure nationally. The fort, with the rest of San Agustin Antiguo, gave St. Augustine a group of historic buildings unmatched elsewhere in this country.

Dr. Michael V. Gannon, distinguished University of Florida history professor, author, and then chairman of the Historic St. Augustine Preservation Board, in 1979 called St. Augustine "the oldest continuously occupied European settlement in the United States, the authentic birthplace of western civilization and Christianity on the North American continent." His description staked a precise claim for St. Augustine. "No other community or locality in the United States can match the variety, age, and complexity of its documented history, archeological resources, and architectural remains; not even Williamsburg or Charleston or Savannah; not Washington, Alexandria, or Boston," he said.

Each of the ruling countries had tried to change St. Augustine. The British took over after 199 years of Spanish rule, and in two years half the town had been torn down for firewood, requiring new replacements. The British renamed the Castillo Fort St. Marks. The Spanish returned in 1784 and worked to rebuild the city. When the United States acquired Florida, it renamed the Castillo Fort Marion (the old Spanish name was not restored until 1942), and some of the new arrivals muttered about the ratty old castles the Spanish had left behind. New arrivals in Florida nearly always had a complaint and a mission to change.

❦ If Florida's colonial history began in St. Augustine with Don Pedro Menéndez de Avilés, fantasy tourism arrived a little more than three centuries later with business tycoon Henry Flagler, who had been a partner of the fabled oilman and financier John D. Rockefeller. Menéndez left Florida a great Castillo; Flagler, among many other things, built a magnificent hotel, the Ponce de Léon, also one of the most historically significant buildings in the state.

Flagler's emergence in Florida delivered public and business birth to the notion that the state was a simple patch of sand that needed to be tricked up into something else to be attractive. Flagler did it with style, but at base his productions still ran counter to the fact that natural Florida by itself was a powerful attraction and, if preserved, might be a better and more lasting investment than any fantasy ever invented.

Flagler introduced fantasy on a scale that exploded a thousand seeds, some of them producing fantasy mutations. While he might never have tolerated such cheap fakery in his hotels and enterprises, out of the fantasy initiatives he loosed came inspiration for penny-scale, copycat mimicry: the tacky roadside zoos and giant snake replicas, the rubber alligators and plastic flamingos, the wire-limbed palm trees, cement oranges, and fabric sharks for which Florida tourism became infamous.

Before the coming of high costs and interstate highways, some (but not all) of the tackiness subsided. Instead there rose the sophisticated fantasies of Disney World and the other "worlds" pitched to tourists, later versions of the grandeurs Flagler invented.

Flagler in 1883 visited the winter resort St. Augustine, the largest East Coast city (pop. 2,300) between Jacksonville and Key West, at a time when Florida was getting serious about incentives for developers. Two years earlier, the state had sold four million acres of land to developer Hamilton Disston, of Philadelphia, for 25 cents an acre. Disston had been introduced to Florida by Henry S. Sanford, a friend who owned land along the St. Johns River. The city of Sanford would bear his name.

Henry B. Plant, another railroad man, visited Jacksonville before the Civil War. In 1883, while Flagler was getting interested in St. Augustine, Plant had similar ideas for Florida's west coast. Railroads, hotels, steamships, and development were on his mind, too. Rebuffed at Cedar Key, Plant moved down to Tampa. He hired Colonel Henry Haines (for whom Haines City would be named). In 1891, Plant built the Tampa Bay Hotel in a grand Spanish-Moorish architectural style that rivaled Flagler's Ponce de León. Plant City was named for him.

Flagler was in his 50s when he came to Florida, immensely wealthy and newly married to his second wife, and certainly aware of both Disston and Plant. The accommodations in St. Augustine were not up to his standards. He began building hotels, and then acquired and enlarged railroads that would bring down from the North larger numbers of guests for them. In the next 17 years, he remade the Florida east coast, pushing the railroad south to Miami and establishing luxury hotels along the way. In another 12 years, he extended that Florida East Coast Railroad across the seas to Key West and died one year later, in 1913. Flagler County, south of St. Augustine, and its county seat, Flagler Beach, were named for him.

In St. Augustine, Flagler's luxurious Ponce de Léon hotel later became Flagler College; his Alcázar Hotel later served as city hall. In St. Augustine and down the east coast he built churches, schools, hospitals, formed land companies and steamship lines. The Flagler hurrah, covering less than 30 years of his life, created the conditions that launched Florida into national prominence.

❦ With some cause, Pensacola has felt like the stepchild of Florida, especially in recognition of its historical distinctions. St. Augustine beats it out as the oldest city on what partisans might call a technicality, Fernandina Beach claims to be the city that has flown the most national flags (eight), Tallahassee has the capitol distinctions, Key West has not only rich history but also the overlay of tropical island ambience, and Cedar Key has unusual history and also the charm of a quaintly isolated fishing village. My many visits to Pensacola persuaded me that it has an honest claim of some sort in all those areas but unfortunately not the best one in any, denying it just and proper recogniton.

Don Tristan de Luna founded Pensacola six years before Menéndez went to St. Augustine, but the Spanish colony was abandoned two years later, giving St. Augustine claim as the first city. The permanent beginning was not until 1696. There were other reasons, principally geography. Out there on the western edge of Florida's Panhandle, closer to Mobile (60 miles) than to Tallahassee (200 miles), closer to New Orleans, Birmingham, and Atlanta than Orlando, the only major Florida city in the Central Time Zone, Pensacola sometimes gets overlooked. It should not be.

Much like St. Augustine, Pensacola has history aplenty: old forts, the Seville Square Historic District, the West Florida Museum of History, the North Hill and Palafox historic districts, the Historic Pensacola Preservation Board, plus a history that features Andrew Jackson as military governor receiving the deed to Florida from Spain on July 17, 1821, in a local park named for King Ferdinand II of Spain. For a half century beginning in 1880, it was a fishing center (the Snapper Capital of the World) as New England fishing fleets moved south to a more benign climate. Among fishermen, Pensacola became known as Hangover Port because, as a civic gesture to fishermen, it set up special "public drunk fines"—lowering the regular fine of $10 to $5 if the drunken one was a fisherman.

《 Two big events elevated Port St. Joe, on the Panhandle Gulf Coast between Panama City and Apalachicola, into a special place in Florida history—a convention at Old St. Joseph in 1838 to give the territory a constitution, quaifying it for statehood, and a great hurricane and tidal wave in 1841, which destroyed the town as it then existed. Port St. Joe grew out of the ruins.

Old St. Joseph, a tragic city that rose and fell in less than one decade (1835–1843), was created following a land dispute in Apalachicola, located at the mouth of the Apalachicola River. Disaffected Apalachicola residents moved 22 miles west and founded a new town, St. Joseph, and within three years had a flourishing cotton port of their own. In 1841 a yellow fever epidemic, believed to have been brought in on a visiting ship, wracked the city. Later a hurricane, with an accompanying tidal surge that rolled huge waves through the town, finished it off, and the survivors moved away.

Charles A. Browne, a guide at the Dr. John Gorrie Museum in Apalachicola (which celebrates his invention of air-conditioning), in the 1970s delighted in telling the story: "It was a wicked city. St. Joseph had 11 saloons and no churches." He pointed out that Port St. Joe, its successor, took no such chances. "They have 11 churches and three saloons."

Jesse Stone, president of the St. Joe Historical Society in 1975, remembered revisionist family stories about the tidal wave disaster. His great-grandfather climbed a tree and stayed there three days to escape the high water.

"My daddy told me about that," Stone said. "He heard it from his daddy, the one who climbed the tree. Everybody said it was a tidal wave, but that isn't what Daddy told me. He said that the water from the bay didn't come over the ridge. Daddy said Granddaddy went up in that tree because of fresh water, not salt. He said there was rain and water backed up on this side of the ridge. He said that was where all the flooding came from in town, not the bay."

Stone conceded margin for confusion and error in personal memories. "Now that's hand-me-down information," he said. "I haven't been able to confirm that anywhere else. Most accounts talk about the tidal wave washing away the town. But that's not what Daddy said."

Stone, then a 55-year-old insurance agent, revered local history and his family's role in it. He elaborated. "Daddy moved down here from Iola (a few miles north) in 1903. He was the first white settler in Port St. Joe. I was among the first white boys born here. That storm finished off what was left of Old St. Joseph. Yellow fever already had scared off most of the people. Vandals had wrecked it. Some of the buildings were dismantled, brick by brick, and taken over to Apalachicola and reassembled.

"Daddy came here and went into the naval stores and turpentine business. That started Port St. Joe. The railroad came along in 1909 or 1910, the city incorporated in 1913, and the St. Joe Paper Co. started operation in 1938 (construction began in 1935), and that made the town."

A 20-mile peninsula or barrier island curls offshore from Cape San Blas and runs west parallel to Port St. Joe and the coast, forming St. Joseph's Bay. On that peninsula is the T. H. Stone Memorial Park. T. H. Stone was Jesse's daddy, the one who told him the stories.

﴾ Arriving strangers created their own little Floridas, some of them only their own backyards, some like Flagler and Plant impacting entire coasts, some making cities that still bear their name. The interesting stories number too many to tell.

A New England seafaring man, Leonard A. Destin, arrived in the 1830s and settled on a narrow peninsula between the Gulf and Choctawhatchee Bay. It became the miracle city and beach resort Destin.

C. B. McClenny built a hotel at a sawmill site west of Jacksonville, trying to lure winter visitors from that city, and the town of Macclenny (changing the spelling) was named for him.

Because a Seattle developer named James Moore bought in 1915 and began to develop 100,000 acres west of Lake Okeechobee, the town of Moore Haven was born.

In 1911 George A. Sebring, a onetime Salvation Army bandmaster and china manufacturer from Ohio, bought 10,000 acres of lakeside wilderness and laid it out like Heliopolis, with streets radiating from a central park like rays from a sun. It became Sebring. In 1996, the founder's grandson, Billy Sebring, was selling used cars north of Sebring on U.S. 27.

J. C. Penney, founder of a chain of department stores, founded Penney Farms. Colonel Harry Titus settled in Florida after the Civil War, and Titusville resulted. Chipley honors Colonel William B. Chipley, railroad promoter.

So many visions, so many reminders. Florida always depended upon uncertain ingredients—the weather, arriving strangers, and peculiar geography—for its well-being. As the strangers came in unending numbers, surprise and swift change inevitably dominated all but the most ancient parts of its story.

Above: Aerial view of Jacksonville, 1970s. Courtesy of the Florida Photographic Collection, Florida State Archives.

Left: This painting of Malcolm Johnson hangs in a local library wing named for him. Courtesy of the *Tallahassee Democrat.* Painting by Ed Jonas.

Above: The beach at Destin before condominiums arrived. Courtesy of the Florida Photographic Collection, Florida State Archives.

Right: Captain John Destin of the family that gave Destin it name. Courtesy of the author.

Left: Sanibel pioneer Clarence Rutland, 1973. Courtesy of the author.

Below: A plane sprays for mosquitoes on Sanibel Island in the early 1970s. Courtesy of the author.

Al Burt at Ding Darling
Wildlife Sanctuary, Sanibel.
Courtesy of the author.

Right: Frog Smith, famed teller of
Florida folktales. Courtesy of the
author.

Below: Lakewood post office, the
highest point in Florida. T. J. Britton,
Jr., and Margaret Britton Richbourg.
Courtesy of the author.

Wakulla Springs. Courtesy of Florida Photographic Collection, Florida State Archives.

Wakulla Springs—the lodge. Courtesy of the author.

Wakulla Springs—an alligator. Courtesy of the author.

John Pennekamp at John Pennekamp Park. Courtesy of the author.

Alison Fahrer standing in front of petrified reef at Windley Key Quarry. Photo by Jim Rubino. Courtesy of the author.

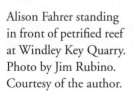

Sunrise over the Indian River. Courtesy of Florida Photographic Collection, Florida State Archives.

Oyster boat in the Apalachicola Bay. Courtesy of the author.

Top left: Hiram Raulerson of Okeechobee. *Miami Herald* photograph by Al Burt.

Left: Okeechobee pioneer Peter Raulerson and his wife, Louisiana. Courtesy of the author.

Top right: Old-time Okeechobee Sheriff William "Pogy Bill" Collins. Courtesy of the author.

Right: Pogy Bill's tombstone. Courtesy of the author.

Below: Castillo de San Marcos, St. Augustine. Courtesy of Florida Photographic Collection, Florida State Archives.

Gamble Rogers in a rocking chair at his home in St. Augustine. Courtesy of the author.

James Hutchinson. Courtesy of the author. Photo by Joan Hutchinson.

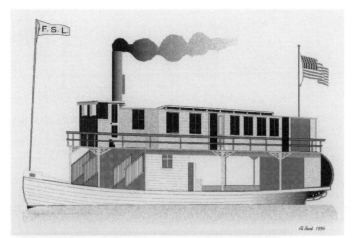

Stern-wheeler steamboat *F. S. Lewis* made Melrose a waterport in 1881. Courtesy of the author.

Trinity Episcopal Church, Melrose. Courtesy of the author.

Above: "The Capitol of Melrose," Chiappini's store. Courtesy of the author. Photo by Gloria Burt.

Left: The driveway at the Burt home in Melrose, 1974. Courtesy of the author.

Pet egret "Biddy" waiting at the backdoor to be fed. Courtesy of the author.

Gloria Burt feeding the pet egret. Courtesy of the author.

Key Westers celebrate sunset at Mallory Dock. Courtesy of the author.

Left: Flach family hog killing in the Panhandle. Courtesy of the author.

Below: View of Key West's Duval Street from the La Concha Hotel in the 1970s. Courtesy of Florida Photographic Collection, Florida State Archives.

 *Crackers, Wry*

While it may be true that a rose is a rose is a rose, as self-proved in Gertrude Stein's poetically mirrored line, in Florida it is not necessarily true that a Cracker is a Cracker. Because the word and its origin are imprecise, so are the uses of it. Cracker has developed so many shades of interpretation, some of them in conflict, that the meaning has been left to the individual. Choose and, just in case there's a misunderstanding, remember to smile when you say it.

A problem arises because a Floridian might speak one version of Cracker and listeners might hear one quite different. In a state where some 40 million tourists visit annually, and where at any one time one-third of the population has been here less than five years, it happens often. That is a pity, for there are grounds of history and custom in Florida for interpreting Cracker simply to mean native birth. While recognizing arguments otherwise, I insist upon using it that way—as a folksy, honorable term for someone born in Florida. We have enough hate words. We do not need to mess up any of the remaining kind ones.

Positive evolution of the Florida term *Cracker* got tangled up with the racial street slur, which is not native to Florida. The problem comes up periodically as Florida restocks its supply of strangers and some of them bring their non-Florida antennae with them, tuned by the negatives of regional history. However, at least in my view, racial segregation in the South and in Florida was not a prejudice practiced only by a low class of citizens whom some now like to call Crackers; it was a flooding shame that saturated the culture. Beyond that, if there were any doubters, the presidential campaigns of Alabama's George Wallace should have been sufficient to prove that race was a national problem. Scapegoating Crackers can't change that now. They were part of a very large crowd.

In 1991, a controversy developed at an elementary school in Sebring, where some parents and students felt it would be derogatory to change the name of the school to Cracker Trail. After much debate, the change was approved—for good and sound reasons of Florida history—because the name had its origin in cattle drives that once passed nearby.

Most accounts suggest the Florida version of *Cracker* was invented as a reference to the state's pioneer cowboys, but nowhere is there a documented record of its beginning. The cowboys cracked long cowhide whips while herding cows, making loud popping noises, and they became known as "crackers." Before, during, and after the Civil War, Florida cowboys drove cattle herds cross-state to railheads and shipping points. "Cracker trail" was a common term. The mid-1860s cattleman Jacob Summerlin was known as the King of the Crackers. History books (such as *Lake Okeechobee* by A. J. Hanna and K. A. Hanna) say the title pleased him greatly.

The concern in Sebring about the name Cracker Trail was a natural and understandable reaction to the racial shading of the word *Cracker,* but the problem was more with the definition than the reality. The settling of that dispute helped promote the Florida definition, but the incident highlighted the problem of usage. If the honest word *Cracker* cannot be used positively and inoffensively, then it will (and should) lose its local status and special Florida meaning, but it deserves better.

Beyond the cowboy origin, other historical speculation has said that the Florida version of Cracker might have come from descriptions of pioneer Floridians pounding or cracking corn to make meal or grits, a diet staple. One suggests it came from the Spanish word *Cuacaros,* meaning Quakers, loosely referring to Florida settlers. Others have traced the word back to Scotland, where it was used to refer to braggarts. All that makes no real difference in Florida. Usage establishes definitions. Florida has justification for picking a good and decent one out of its own history of usage.

Florida did not invent the racist shadings, but they were applied as Florida developed, principally by exploitive big-city writers who saw the state as an exotically backward place and felt compelled to emphasize the grotesque side of reality for the amusement of the readers back home in "civilization," where much the same problems went unrecognized or undetailed.

Popularity of the racist interpretation especially blossomed as a shorthand epithet for bigots during the civil rights wars of this century. Dictionaries picked that up, without reference to the separate Florida strain of meaning (which probably was considered apologist). The racist definition contested the homegrown definition of Cracker.

Periodically, someone who grew up with negative definitions of *Cracker* would write me an incensed letter attacking my benign use of the word Cracker in a column for *The Miami Herald*. My standard reply: I understand your view, and I have the same disrespect for people of that character as you, but I remain persuaded that Florida has earned the right to consider it a positive term. Beyond that, I would conclude, that is how I choose to continue using it.

The 1939 book, *Florida: A Guide to the Southernmost State* (New York: Oxford University Press, 1939, p. 128), a standard for its time, compiled and written by the Federal Writers' Project of the Works Project Administration, stated: "The Cracker, a pioneer backwoods settler of Georgia and Florida, has come to be known as a gaunt, shiftless person *but originally the term meant simply a native, regardless of his circumstances* [italics added]."

Stetson Kennedy, a distinguished writer, folklorist, and native (born in Jacksonville in 1916), was one of a half-dozen state editors employed by the WPA to produce that book. Later, he wrote nationally sensational books exposing the Ku Klux Klan and Jim Crow laws in the United States. In his elder years he became the statesman and conscience of Florida folk life, emphasizing its variety and ethnic richness and avoiding concentration on any one aspect of it.

In 1984 he wrote a letter to the Florida Folklore Society, of which he later became president: "Folk culture . . . is the boiled-down pot likker of life . . . the joys and sorrows of the group . . . the hard-earned lessons of living . . . handed down from generation to generation." (Pot likker [liquor] is a Southern expression that describes the rich juices boiled out of turnip or collard greens.)

The WPA group's collections remained the most significant body of work on Florida folklore. In speeches, essays, and conversation, Kennedy would recall old Florida expressions that could be called Crackerisms. A favorite: "When you ain't got no education, you got to use your *brain*." Another noted slyly that "the sun don't shine on the same dog's tail all the time."

Cracker humor honored the old ways. One businessman in Central Florida, whose mother had been a teacher, told me about encountering one of her former students. With great sincerity, the man delivered his highest praise. "I loved your mama," he said. "She learnt me English."

Nothing captures the flavors of old Florida better than the wry comments of Crackers. A Cracker thinks it's perfectly proper to sum up his visit to the Florida legislature with a remark that "those fellows sound like a bunch of mockingbirds that were raised in an outhouse." A Cracker—noting that conventional progress has resulted in declining quality of air and water, and in risks to certain foods—would find kinship in the message that author Herman Melville wove into the great novel *Moby Dick*, that businesslike madness sometimes passes in the world as reason.

In 1982, Dr. David L. Closson, a tall, dapper African-American, became director of the Florida folk-life program. He arrived with a Ph.D. from the University of Pennsylvania, one earring, a drooping mustache, and an affection for African drums picked up during two years of Peace Corps Service in Idi Amin's Uganda. While toting up his first four months on the job for me, he confessed one special surprise. "Another thing I learned," he said, "was the use of the word *Cracker*. I would never have used that word before, because in Northern parlance it had the same pejorative ring as nigger. Whereas, here, it's a positive term."

Erskine Caldwell, whose 1930s novels (*Tobacco Road, God's Little Acre,* and eventually 53 others) elevated the Crackers of Georgia into nationally disgusting caricatures, was a man whose distaste for redneckism was legendary. He once described himself to me as a Florida Cracker. Sensitive, worldly, patrician, frustrated that he no longer could produce major novels, he was living in Dunedin then, in 1976, with his fourth wife. He commented that Tobacco Road had been blacktopped and that the descendants of Jeeter Lester and Ty Ty Walden (characters in the books) had moved to the cities to feed at what he called the welfare troughs. For him, the Florida Cracker had no relationship to Ty Ty and Jeeter. His definition was more liberal than most: "There are two kinds of people living in

Florida," he said. "There are those who live here six months and those who live here year-round. You don't have to be born here to be a Cracker. Anybody who stays here year-round, through these long summers, becomes a Cracker."

Another man known as the King of the Crackers, and proud of it, was Wisconsin-born Lawrence E. Will. He came to Florida at age 20, fresh out of a Washington, D.C., high school. His father, Dr. Thomas E. Will, a Harvard graduate, former college president (Kansas State Agricultural College), and former secretary of the American Forestry Association, visited the Everglades in 1910. He bought land and the family moved there in 1913. The Wills established the town of Okeelanta south of Lake Okeechobee. "We were the first ones ever to farm in the sawgrass country," Lawrence, then 83, told me in 1976.

He remembered his first look at what was then a primitive land. "There was a dense screening of custard apple trees that grew from the edge of the lake on the south and the east sides. It came back two or three miles. Where the trees ended, the sawgrass started and ran on down the state a hundred miles. This sawgrass was higher than your head and as thick as it could grow. You couldn't walk through it. The leaves were triangular, kind of V-shaped, and grew straight up. They were just as sharp as razors, and had very fine teeth on each of the edges. Farming that sawgrass land was different from anything else. It took one man one month to clear one acre."

For the next half century, Lawrence Will roamed and worked in the Everglades, making Belle Glade his home in 1927 and acquiring a practical knowledge of that area matched by few. He farmed, helped build the levees around the lake, helped run a dredge that dug canals, raised cattle and sugarcane, worked in a Fort Lauderdale boatyard, and ran a passenger and freight boat line from there to the lake, helped build the Tamiami Trail (from Miami to Naples), lived through hurricanes, served on the Belle Glade town council, and was bus agent for 26 years and fire chief for 30. For Will, the entire cluster of lake communities—including Clewiston, Moore Haven, Pahokee, Okeechobee, Canal Point, Port Mayaca—was his home.

He accumulated stories that had a blend of science fiction and Cracker tall tales. He could tell you about the time his father promoted chicken farming at Okeelanta, arguing that there was an unending supply of natural food—water hyacinths—for the hens to eat. He had stories about the great cracks that would form in the black muck when it dried, about nose-to-nose encounters with cottonmouth moccasins, about mosquitoes swarming so thickly that they extinguished lamps, about a time when the marketing of egret plumes was so common a business that they could be sold to the department store Burdines. Will knew the human parade around the great lake, a carousel of characters: Indians, cowboys, catfishermen, outlaws and lawmen, empire builders, migrants, farmers, bootleggers—most, in his eyes, Crackers.

At 68, he decided to write the stories that he had lived. He put them into the conversational style of the old-time Crackers, a language that later arrivals had trouble interpreting. "I wrote like the Crackers talked in those days," he said. "The Crackers were uneducated but I can't say that they were ignorant. They weren't. I associated with 'em and I appreciated knowing 'em. They were my friends and companions."

The books, with that primitive style and a historically accurate pioneer viewpoint that included the prejudices of the time, were published by the Great Outdoors Company of St. Petersburg. *Okeechobee Hurricane* (1961) dealt with the hurricanes of 1926 and 1928 and was dedicated to Herbert Hoover, who built the dike around the lake following the 1928 hurricane. There followed the *Cracker History of Okeechobee* (1964), *Okeechobee Boats and Skippers* (1965), *Okeechobee Catfishing* (also 1965), *A Dredgeman of Cape Sable* (1967), and *Swamp to Sugar Bowl: Pioneer Days in Belle Glade* (1968). Will died in 1977, but his photographs and files were preserved in the Lawrence E. Will Museum at the Belle Glade Library.

True to the Florida pattern (migration affects all), a refugee from Rochester, N.Y., adopted the Florida Crackers in the 1930s and became their literary godmother, probably their greatest and best-known champion. Marjorie Kinnan Rawlings moved to Cross Creek, Florida, in 1928 and in the following years produced a series of books (including *The Yearling*, a Pulitzer Prize–winner; *Cross Creek*, a book of essays; and more) that embraced the Crackers as honest folk who lived in harmony with their surroundings. Her husband, the gentlemanly Norton Baskin, called himself an Alabama Cracker.

The first publication (1931) of Rawlings's Florida work, entitled *Cracker Chidlings*, dealt with Cracker peculiarities and began a long and distinguished career that was marked by its "missionary zeal," as her biographer, Gordon E. Bigelow, put it in *Frontier Eden* (Gainesville: University Press of Florida, 1966), to portray Crackers as gentle, even noble primitives whose parents or grandparents had migrated from Georgia or the Carolinas. She saw them, Bigelow said, as intelligent and sensitive folk who had their own code of conduct.

Rawlings drew criticism for this, but she persisted and to a large degree, I think, was responsible for rescuing the evolution of *Cracker* as a word with positive Florida meaning. According to *Selected Letters of Marjorie Kinnan Rawlings* (edited by Gordon E. Bigelow and Laura V. Monti, among other critics of her viewpoint was the editor of the *Ocala Evening Star,* who wrote a locally righteous editorial denouncing her as an outsider who did not understand what Crackers were like. In a letter, she delivered a blistering defense of her work and the Crackers, praising their "primal quality" and calling them "delightful."

Two of Rawlings' real-life characters were the Boyt brothers of Citra, a Marion County village six miles south of where the Cross Creek road joins U.S. 301. The Boyt brothers were examples of Self-Rising Crackers, a term borrowed from Cracker kitchens. Self-rising flour came with all the ingredients needed to make the bread rise. With other flour, you had to add stuff. A Self-Rising Cracker was one who "pulled himself up by his own bootstraps," who succeeded largely by his own efforts and skills.

In 1975 I visited the Boyts at their ancient roadside service station in Citra. By then Henry Boyt, called Gator, was 88 and his brother, Raymond, 74. Both still seemed pleased at the continued celebrity that the Rawlings books had created for them.

Gator chewed Beech-Nut tobacco, kept the trouser legs of his overalls rolled up halfway to the knees, giving his calves a nice tan, and spit carefully. Raymond had built the corrugated tin structure a half century earlier, when U.S. 301 was a dirt road that floundered in the marsh a half mile to the north. In the old days, Gator joined his brother at the gas station and garage whenever his hunting, farming, and duties as Marion County deputy sheriff would permit. When I saw them, they sat out front of the old gas station, as calm as a pair of old hunters in a deer blind. They tilted back their chairs next to the Coke machine and whiled away the time watching the traffic roar by on a U. S. 301 that had become four-laned.

"Me and Raymond'll sit it out right here," said Gator. "We don't worry about anything except our health." He was a widower but had three daughters living in the area. "They call me Gator because I used to handle gators. I'd kill 'em and sell their hides. I hunted 'em and bought 'em, done both. Shot 'em with a .38 and a shotgun. They tell ya gators won't hurt ya, but they will. They're just mean. Big alligators'll catch ya and eat ya. I know enough about 'em to know that a big old hungry alligator is one of the dangerousest things that you can be around in the water."

The Boyt brothers worked hard all their lives. Raymond could remember taking only one vacation, a brief one. "That was when I got married, 54 years ago," he said. "Took my day off and stayed home." He smiled. "Still married to the same woman."

The Boyts left Citra once to go with a local employer who opened a business in Fellsmere (near Vero Beach). They didn't like it and after six months came back to Citra. "Never did travel much," said Raymond, lighting a Picayune cigarette. Gator nodded agreement. "I been as far north as Jacksonville and as far south as Miami. That's a pretty place. Lots of people," he said.

Three years after they first established their gas station, they met Marjorie Kinnan Rawlings. "A very fine, intelligent lady," Raymond said. "She used to bring her Oldsmobile over here. Went to trading with us. People thought she was just as nice as she could be. Didn't make any difference that she came from New York. She didn't know a lot about this section when she came, but she learned. I been over to her house. Gave me a drink of moonshine. Good stuff, made right around here. She liked a little drink now and then, but she was a nice lady."

The Boyt brothers were two of Rawlings's storied Crackers. She wrote about going to their garage for help, and she described their frogging business, which once supplied frog legs to restaurants from Chicago to New York. The Boyts hired 35 or 40 frog hunters who would fan out through the lakes area, gigging frogs or capturing them bare-handed, and bring their catch back to Citra. The Boyts would load the frogs into barrels and ship them out. "Shipped out as many as five barrels a day," Gator said.

The novelist Pat Smith of Merritt Island, whose books, including *Forever Island* and *A Land Remembered* concentrated on Florida, wrote an admiring essay "What Is a Florida Cracker?" in whch he called Crackers "my kind of folks." Nixon Smiley, respected Florida specialist for *The Miami Herald* in the 1960s, entitled his column "A Cracker Viewpoint." Ray Washington, a fourth-generation Floridian, in the 1970s wrote a column for the *Gainesville Sun* called "Cracker Florida." Washington defined a Cracker as a native Floridian, usually of rural upbringing. In his book *Florida: A Short History*, author Michael Gannon said that *Cracker* was a "sobriquet for native Floridians." A *Florida Living Magazine* column by editor Douglas Cifers periodically carries a feature called "Cracker Kudos," congratulating Florida achievements. The publisher, John Paul Jones, Jr., proudly calls himself a Cracker. The magazine has published a book titled *Cracker Girl* by Nadine Strickland Dixon (Gainesville, Fla.: Florida Living Magazine, 1994) extolling early Florida life.

Dr. Clark I. Cross, a University of Florida (sometimes known as the Cracker Citadel) professor and geographer, studied Cracker culture in the 1970s. He stated the case for evolution of the term. "It is a state of mind, a self-sufficiency, an attitude of independence," he said. "The Crackers were good people, just different. As life has become easier, the Cracker has become more like everyone else. He didn't disappear. He assimilated." Cross liked to tell a story that had a flavor Crackers enjoyed. In the old days at Florida football games, when the stadium crowds roared, a bull gator in a lake south of the campus often would answer with a roar of its own. That's old-time Florida.

Native Floridian Bob Graham (two-term governor, two-term U.S. Senator), perhaps Florida's most popular politician in the 1990s, understood about Cracker identification. During his statewide campaigns, bumper stickers appeared on cars around the state proudly identifying the drivers as "Graham Crackers."

In the 1990s, Florida governor Lawton Chiles, a native of Lakeland and growing political legend (three-time U.S. senator, two-time governor)— put on a coonskin cap and proudly called himself a He-coon and a Cracker. The He-Coon (male raccoon) in Cracker lore ranks as a fierce fighter. Chiles presented his Cracker credentials this way: loyal to family, friends, and state; concerned about the unfortunate; ready to work cooperatively to solve problems; a tad suspicious of outsiders. Occasionally, as governor, Chiles ran into constituents who did not understand the Florida meaning of Cracker. His folksy explanations smoothed it over.

Especially notable was Chiles's 1994 campaign for reelection against Republican Jeb Bush, who sometimes appeared to be jarred by Chiles's He-coon posturing and Cracker-style wisdom. For example, in one televised debate between them, after Bush noted that Chiles trailed in the polls, Chiles gave this surprising reply: "The He-coon walks just before the light of day."

The stunned look on young Jeb Bush's face went into the history books. It was a face that wondered just what this old man was talking about this time, a face struck speechless for just a moment by the strange Florida Creole he had just heard, one puzzling whether this was senility or some kind of backwoods riddle. If Bush understood that Chiles was saying that his candidacy got stronger as election night drew closer, it didn't show. Bush hesitated; Chiles smiled and won the debate. Chiles had the enabling Cracker credentials to try it, and he had the He-coon innards to pull it off. It might have been the last true Cracker hurrah in state politics. If so, it was a good one.

Will Addison used to describe himself as "a full-blooded Cracker." Addison, born in 1880, had classic Florida memories. At age 95 he could recall the days when he sold egret plumes ("a dollar each") and hunted alligators ("a six-foot gator brought 65 cents"). The law made him quit.

"I seen my daddy bring two corn sacks full [of egret plumes], and he'd take one on the front of his saddle and tie one up behind and go to Kissimmee and sell 'em," he said. "One time he got paid in silver dollars. Have you seen those 25-pound shot sacks they used to buy to load their [gun] shells in? He had two or three of them big old shot sacks full of silver dollars."

Addison once raised cattle on open range, but a fence law and slaughter regulations complicated that for him. He once fished Lake Okeechobee with giant trotlines, once built his own house with pine logs taken from the forest, once grew oranges in the little grove around his house and sold them directly to truckers—all since prohibited or at least hindered by regulations.

Addison's grandfather left South Carolina before the Civil War and moved near Arcadia, where he was a cattleman. Addison's father told him about driving 2,700 cattle from Arcadia across Indian trails to the area of Fort Lauderdale, where they would be shipped first to Key West and then to Cuba.

For supplies, the Addison family used to travel to Fort Pierce by oxcart (a three-day trip), or over to Basinger to meet the steamboats coming down the Kissimmee River. As a boy, because there was no kerosene, he held burning lightwood splinters up so that his mother could see to cook and wash dishes. "Tar'd drop out of them. I'd drop it on my feet. Sometimes I'd be a-nodding, and Maw'd say, 'Wake up there and snuff that light out'."

For men like Will Addison, Cracker was an honorable description. He boasted of it. He would have been astonished to hear someone suggest anything else.

I have been reading about Crackers and observing them all my life. Long ago I discovered with regret that any positive use of the term might draw argument, if not anger. Historic citations, recent or ancient, will not settle that argument. It depends upon viewpoint. Florida has solid reasons for preferring the kindly, folklorish meaning of the word *Cracker,* and I hope that will survive. I use it that way, I recommend it to all Floridians. Use it with affection and do what you can to save (or rehabilitate, if you prefer) the good word *Cracker.*

Miracle Folk among the Mangroves

For a man only forty-one years old, Father Michael Mooney knew a lot about the human condition. Mooney was one of those quiet heroes of Florida. He went about his business routinely doing things according to conscience, setting large examples. He identified, in a way that only personal experience made possible, the mystery of prejudice. He found it had something to do with fear, the instinct of self-preservation. Only the brave could overcome it.

Mooney grew up in Ireland, where his father and grandfather in the North could not vote because they did not own property and could not own property because they were Catholic. The ancient struggle there, he told me one day in 1980 at his church in Pensacola, fundamentally was more a conflict between English Loyalists and Irish Nationalists than between Catholics and Protestants. His uncles and cousins had been killed in it.

There were times as a young man, he said, when he puzzled about the situation. "Why would anyone treat me different because I'm a Catholic?" he would ask. Even as an older man who understood better the subtleties of prejudice, mystery remained. "In Ireland there is no great love for the

English, you know," he said in his distinctly accented voice. "It is something I can't explain. They are like everybody else. There are English Catholics and English priests. It has nothing to do with Christianity, and it is not so much anything English, but there is something."

Because a need existed, Mooney in the 1960s volunteered to serve the church in the U.S. South. Those were the violent years of the civil rights struggles. He was sent to St. Joseph's in Pensacola, a church in the old section of town, principally black. In the South, where he had no personal background, the mystery of prejudice deepened. He could not believe the hatred that existed. "Why would you treat a man differently because he has black skin?" he asked, and realized that essentially it was the same question he had asked in Ireland. In Florida, the puzzle continued to repeat itself.

From a distance, he had been familiar with the multi-ethnic turmoil of Miami. When a trickle of refugees from the Far East began to come to Pensacola, he volunteered to help. The problems at first were not dramatic, but they reinforced his perception of prejudice as a defensive instinct.

"There is prejudice everywhere, of course," he said. "It is a common denominator within the human that there has to be one class over another. We make distinctions because of our greed, our need for superiority. I'm better than you are, and my group is superior to your group and my class better than your class. We should not forget, either, that refugees have the same instincts. It is easy to talk about but not easy to acknowledge that each of us is prejudiced to one degree or another. We cover it up. You say, 'I'm not really a prejudiced person,' but when it comes to something you really care about—your neighborhood, your living habits, your children—you resist. You say, 'Well, it's just not good and it has nothing to do with prejudice,' but it does."

Father Mooney, wearily philosophical, described the moral struggle as one that required the attitude of the long-distance runner, patiently enduring and persistent, or maybe that of an alcoholic whose battle had to be renewed each day but never could be won.

Occasionally, he was surprised. The Lions Club once asked him to speak to them about refugee problems. He arrived for the restaurant meeting a bit late, went directly to the podium and spoke earnestly for 20 minutes, after which he discovered he was in the wrong room. He had been talking to the Jaycees, not the Lions. "Those people had no idea in the world what I was doing, but afterward they took up a collection for the refugees anyway," he said.

Sometimes, the surprises have not been so good. One day he noticed at the cemetery that a life-size crucifix, made of dark metal, had become a bit weather-beaten. "I had some black paint, so I touched it up. I was not trying to make a black Jesus; it already was black," he explained.

Father Mooney went back to the cemetery a few days later and found that the Jesus figure had been repainted white. "Very white," he said, "and it was not a sloppy job. It was not the work of vandals. It was very carefully done."

He reconsidered the dilemma thus presented. "Jesus was not a black man," he said. "For that matter, he was not white, either. Yet in our theology, our philosophy, he could be any color. What difference does it make? The statue wasn't painted black for the sake of being black. That was the color of the metal. It had been that way a long time."

The incident did not surprise Father Mooney. He knew that something similar could happen in Ireland, in Pensacola, in Miami, or almost anywhere else in the world. The problem was human, not geographical. What still puzzled him, after all those years, was why.

He decided what to do. "I am looking for some more black paint," he said.

The miracle folk of Florida take their cue from the nature of the state, from the wonders that occur so naturally and perform so efficiently that they sometimes go unnoticed or underappreciated. Mangroves anchor the shore, holding beaches against the erosion of tides and storms; sea oats, elegantly slim and tall and festive, spread their roots into the sand and keep the dunes in place; alligators create water holes that nurture other creatures during droughts; gopher tortoises burrow into sandhills, making sheltering caves. So it goes in Florida. Whatever else might be happening, miraculous things and miraculous people still occur in common places, serving unobtrusively with heroic purpose. Those unhailed ones, most of whom neither won headlines nor made the marketplace sing, became my favorites.

Henry L. Twine of St. Augustine was one. Twine knew in the most practical of ways about those mysteries that Father Mooney pondered. He sprang from one of Florida's most historically distinctive families, yet he had the peculiar experience of not enjoying until 1964 as full a range of freedom and respect as an illustrious ancestor had in 1816. This did not embitter Twine. Freedom for his family never had been a casual thing. None of them ever had it securely enough to take it for granted. Twine won it his own way, with deliberation and dignity.

Even in St. Augustine, a city of historical superlatives, his story was extraordinary. Not until 1978, when Twine was 55 years old, did a fuller perspective begin to develop within which his family could be appreciated for its contributions to history. That year, the Historic St. Augustine Preservation Board began a study to identify all the cultural resources of the community. The Twine family was among them.

Their American family roots began with a teenaged Jamaican slave named Antonio Proctor, brought to this country as a servant of a British officer before the American Revolution. I first talked with Twine (a career postal service employee with 29 years service at the time) in 1981 and looked at the research on his family history. At that time not all the dates and places were certain, but young Tony (as historical documents referred to Proctor) apparently had been with the British in Boston at the time of the famous Tea Party and also at Lexington when "the shot heard round the world" was fired, starting the American Revolution.

The firm of Panton, Leslie & Co. brought Proctor to St. Augustine about 1800, during the second period of Spanish rule, which had begun in 1784. Proctor so distinguished himself while serving the Spanish governor, acting as messenger and informal ambassador to the Indians as well as interpreter, that in 1816 he was established as a free mulatto and given 185 acres of land near St. Augustine. He remained there after the 1821 treaty made Florida a U.S. territory.

Under U.S. rule, Proctor continued to distinguish himself. Governor William P. Duval described him as a "man of truth and integrity . . . [whose] services were invaluable to the United States in the management of the Florida Indians at a period when no other person could have preserved the peace of the country."

In 1824, about the time Tallahassee was founded, Proctor moved there and continued his government service. When he died in 1855, at age 112, the *Florida Sentinel* published his lengthy obituary with a display and praise usually accorded only the most prominent white citizens.

Proctor, however, had lived long enough to see how fragile freedom can be. His son, George, an independent contractor in Tallahassee, went broke during the Panic of 1837, a depression. Unable to recover, George mortgaged his family (these were slavery times) so that he could go to California during the 1849 gold rush and recover his fortune. He did not have success, and the family, including sons John and George Jr., were sold into slavery.

After the Civil War, the two sons, as freedmen and Republicans, served in the Florida legislature. Since then, other descendants of Antonio Proctor have succeeded in education, medicine, and the ministry. Henry L. Twine's grandfather, Henry L. Proctor, moved to St. Augustine around 1900 and with other relatives helped establish the First Colored (later changed to Christian) Methodist Episcopal Church in 1909.

Twine, a seventh-generation descendant of Proctor, was born in 1923, when the Jim Crow laws establishing segregation were in force. Though the racial atmosphere in St. Augustine was peaceful even if patronizing, law and custom enforced inequality, and Twine grew up feeling himself to be less free than Antonio Proctor had been.

"As long as we were docile, stayed in our place, didn't ask for anything, nobody paid any attention to us," Twine said. "But when we started making certain demands, this troubled the waters."

Early in the 1960s, Twine and other black leaders in St. Augustine began pressing for basic rights. They wanted to eat in the restaurants, drink at the public water fountains, use the rest rooms, sleep in the motels. They felt they made little progress until they appealed to Dr. Martin Luther King, Jr., for help. As a result, Dr. King's nonviolent campaign focused on St. Augustine and drew violent responses that surprised even Twine. "We knew there would be trouble, but we didn't know it would go so far," Twine said. There were beatings, jailings (Twine's wife, Katherine, said she went to jail so often that she kept her suitcase packed), fire-bombings of houses, multiple rounds of weapons fired into homes, losses of jobs, encounters with attack dogs.

"King had something new," Twine said. "Blacks had never gotten in the street and marched like that here. They'd always been afraid. We'd always been taught to run get under the house, get under the bed when the police came. He showed us a new way. We never fought back, never did anything. We got beat, got stomped, but we won. It was a price we had to pay. It was just like Biblical times. We were offering ourselves as living sacrifices."

The first black slaves introduced into what is now the United States came to St. Augustine in 1580. A fort manned by runaway black slaves, Fort Mose, helped defend the city in the 1750s. Antonio Proctor earned his freedom in the early 1800s, and then his sons lost it. Henry L. Twine, Proctor's direct descendant, won it back in 1964.

Unlike some, he stayed in St. Augustine during and after the violent parts of the struggle. He endured the backlash and finally enjoyed the sweet reward of seeing a great many of his rights dreams come true. He lived in a house designed by a great-uncle. He went to a church founded by his grandfather. He had a secure job. His son had been quarterback on the football team at an integrated local high school. At one Proctor family reunion, a big event, the mayor and the sheriff and the county commissioners turned out to honor the oldest documented black family in the nation's oldest city.

Once we sat down in his historic home on Palmo Street in St. Augustine and talked about all that. The house was full of history books, scrapbooks, and hopes. "Things may not be perfect even now," he said, "but they're better."

They're better, and Florida is better, because he had conviction, bravery, understanding. Twine, a Florida folk hero, died in September 1994.

For Nathaniel Pryor Reed, a conservation gladiator and jet-setting businessman, environment was the thing that put him among the miracle folk. His case was somewhat different from others, though. Headlines did come for him, but they never were quite what they should have been; the marketplace sang about his family enterprises but not his public-service work.

For nearly a half century, he patiently fought the exploiters wherever he encountered them, from the corridors of Washington to the swamps of the Everglades. He was a Republican who earned the respect of almost all, including Democrats.

The distinguished former Democratic governor LeRoy Collins—himself one of Florida's miracle folk—described Reed this way in 1982: "I have never known a citizen of our state who I feel deserves greater respect than Nat does. . . . He is put together with solid blocks of virtue. He is deeply sensitive to what is right and good. . . . He has become one of our country's greatest conservationists."

At six feet five inches, Nat Reed was not a man you could overlook, but there was a chance you could get used to him, the way you might get used to the sight of a magnificently tall pine or stunning Florida sunsets. So steady and so strong was he in the cause of Florida that there was danger he might be taken for granted, not appreciated for his rarity. He was involved with distinction in every environmental issue. His advice and counsel have been sought from California to Georgia. In 1996, approaching his mid-60s, he still remained on the frontline.

Once, in the 1960s, he went before the water board and protested the loosing of silt-laden waters into the St. Lucie River. So vociferously did he argue that he was thrown out of the meeting. He came back years later to serve not only as a board member of the South Florida Water Management District but also as its chairman.

A favorite story about Reed involves a hamburger joint. After one long, wrangling water board meeting that went hours past the dinner hour, Reed and some others decided to go out and eat. Nothing was open except a fast-food place, and so there they went, but Reed was nervous about it. "I've never been in one of these places," he told John Wodraska, a friend and fellow water management official. "You'll have to show me what to do." They had hamburgers. Reed was astounded at how good the meal tasted. He raved about it. "This is wonderful," he said. "I must compliment the chef." Though the others advised him it was not necessary, Reed insisted upon going to the kitchen and thanking a young assembly-line hamburger cooker.

In 1981, after having served two Republican administrations as assistant secretary of the Department of the Interior, he challenged the new secretary of that department, James Watt, in the bluntest language. In a speech to the Sierra Club in San Francisco, he called Watt's approach "lame-brained, outmoded."

In 1987, he founded the 1000 Friends of Florida, an organization dedicated to promoting intelligent growth standards and to acting as watchdog for their enforcement. He has been prominent in the National Audubon Society and the Nature Conservancy. His other honors and achievements have been many, perhaps best symbolized by the 1994 Calder Award, which hailed him as "a national giant in environmental protection for over three decades."

"It's like ballroom dancing," Reed once said of his unending battles for the environmental cause—"one step forward, two steps back."

Closest to his heart, probably, have been the Everglades. From nearby Jupiter Island, where Nat lived on an island bought by his father in 1932 and developed into an exclusive resort, he kept a constant eye on what his friend Marjory Stoneman Douglas called the "River of Grass." Four presidents, six governors, and six secretaries of the interior came and went while Reed crusaded for the Everglades (our "most ecologically valuable pool of water"). His friend Art Marshall, the fiery environmental evangelist who was careful with praise, considered him a giant. Reed, Marshall, and Douglas—all miracle folk—belong in any Everglades hall of fame.

In later years, Reed focused on population growth and water. "I continue to be astonished by the numbers. Would you have guessed that, over the last 10 years, Florida's growth rate has surpassed that of China and India?" he said in 1993.

"Having grown up in a far different Florida, a Florida of open spaces, of unlimited natural resources, I am totally terrified by the demands of nearly six million South Floridians . . . with an estimate of four million more coming in less than 10 years," he told the National Audubon Society a year later.

Speaking to the Georgia Conservancy in 1995, he suggested that state ought to learn from Florida's mistakes. The great lesson, he said, "is that we dictated to nature, instead of learning from it." He added: "Florida's future . . . is truly about the control of water. Water will control land use. . . . Water will control people (how many can fit). . . . Water will control our economy."

Classically, Reed the outdoorsman compared Florida to an African water hole—where "all the animals come to drink with one eye on the water and one eye on each other."

Listen, cheer, appreciate an extraordinary Floridian.

The Carr family had heart roots in Florida, not native but the adoptive kind, that involved migration—coming in from the cold, as so many others have, and becoming deeply and lovingly attached to the realities of the state.

Archie was born in Alabama and grew up in Georgia, and after high school the family moved down to the heart of Florida country near Umatilla and the Ocala forest. He was the quiet part of the family. By the time he died in 1987, he had become a world-class herpetologist as well as a distinguished University of Florida professor, without great hurrah.

Marjorie Harris and her family were weather migrants, Snowbirds. The Harrises moved to southwest Florida from New England, because her father wanted to work and retire in a warmer place. She grew up in what were the semitropical wilds of Bonita Springs and loved it as Archie did the scrub. She created political tremors.

They met at the University of Florida in the 1930s, married and made their home in historic Micanopy near an alligator pond, producing five children who helped them bend the state's history in beneficial ways. Few other names have such distinguished auras as theirs.

In 1982 *Audubon* magazine praised the Carrs as people who had identified "what matters most" and added: "They have coped with the realities of the modern world, brought up their children decently, and had the guts to make some enemies along the way."

Archie's feel for the natural world turned him into a sensitive writer, and he accumulated many honors. His quietly dedicated life made permanent impressions. Marjorie, a biology major who did her masters thesis on the large-mouthed black bass, in 1962 took up the cause of the Ocklawaha River, a North Central Florida stream so naturally beautiful that it had mythical qualities. The river was being threatened then by one of the old conquer-and-develop dreams—a cross-Florida canal. That dream first found voice in the 16th-century time of Pedro Menéndez, the Spanish colonizer. In my time, North Florida businessmen saw it as a boost for the economy.

She was more blunt than Archie, perhaps more practical about the political world, but still avoided the zealotry that backfired on some environmental true believers. She used a blend of science and communications skills to pursue her goals in an aggressive yet nonantagonistic way. The core of her strategy was a science-based organization she founded in 1969—Florida Defenders of the Environment—which produced persuasive reasons of cost as well as environmental damage for not building the canal.

Each time the canal issue seemed overwhelmed by FDE facts, it would revive again. As this went on for a quarter century or more, Marjorie became a skilled political lobbyist and propagandist for her worthy cause. President Nixon stopped work on the canal in 1971, but state and federal authorization remained on the books. The state finally erased those, and in 1990 Congress did also.

Still left was one major piece to the Ocklawaha preservation—the Rodman Dam, built in 1968 as part of the canal project. It flooded a portion of the river and created a lake that fishermen loved. FDE scientists argued that the dam cost too much tax money to maintain, said that the lake was declining and would continue to wane as a fishery. They wanted the dam removed so that the Ocklawaha could flow freely again. Many fishermen wanted to keep Rodman intact. It seemed inevitable that Marjorie and the FDE and a free-flowing Ocklawaha would win, but the battle went on, year after year.

The Carrs lived for 40 years by the side of a sinkhole pond. Archie named the pond Wewa, the Seminole Indian word for water. The pond and the Micanopy retreat gave the Carrs a private dimension to their knowledge of Florida. Wewa became a Cracker base that brought human perspective to Archie's international studies. He traveled from Costa Rica to Africa, producing many books, including *Ulendo: Travels of a Naturalist In and Out of Africa* and *The Windward Road,* and bringing in prestigious awards and honors.

Archie was remarkable in almost every way—a good and kind family man, an extraordinary scientist with all the discipline that implies, a brilliantly skilled writer brimming with whimsy and imagination.

"It's not that more happens around Archie," Marjorie once explained to someone marveling at his ability to find compelling drama in life all around him. "It's that he's extra perceptive. He sees more."

In his writing, Archie poked into the wonders of Florida with a quiet persistence, examining frog songs, gator fleas, cut-bait fishing (with dynamite), alligator dining habits, the spiritual force of Spanish moss, and much, much more. In her late years Marjorie, fighting off poor health, culled Archie's writings into a final gem of a book, *A Naturalist in Florida: A Celebration of Eden,* published by Yale University Press.

The Carrs, Archie and Marjorie, with their words and deeds heroically elevated the wonders of Florida into the public conscience.

℘ Gamble Rogers, the entertainer, championed Florida with a smile and a song, with love and caricature. He seemed ever on the edge of major stardom, wildly popular among the Cracker-loving folklore set in Florida, never quite breaking through so spectacularly on the national stage. Even while he stood on a stage hypnotically singing story-songs that evange-lized for the soul of native Florida, Gamble delivered humanity and mys-tery. With humor, he mythologized Crackers and poked fun at Snow-birds.

In 1991, then a fifty-five-year-old grandfather, he elevated his life with an act of genuine heroism. He drowned in the surf off Flagler Beach while trying to save a Canadian tourist from the same fate. His ironic end, com-ing as he tried to rescue one of those tourists whose foibles he exploited, belonged among the epic poems he created and loved to recite.

Rogers had become a small spur in the hide of conventional Florida, a joke-cracking catalyst for the enhancement of heritage and identity. To realize its dreams, Florida needed a state full of people like him, and that made his passing something worthy of lament.

He was one of those essentially shy, bookish people who astonished himself by becoming an entertainer—so successful at it that he once played the old *Ed Sullivan Show* (as one of the Serendipity Singers). Later, as a folklorist-singer-musician he regularly performed in nightclubs and on college campuses across the country. He contributed essays to Na-tional Public Radio and for years was the star attraction at the annual Florida Folklife Festival in White Springs.

His act was memorable. On stage, he had the look of a zealot. His long, thin black hair would switch this way and that. His eyes would light up with the intensity of a John Brown raging at a slave auction. His long arms stretched out and grappled with the air. When he spoke, it was an athletic act. Multisyllablic words tumbled out like Olympic gymnasts. ("Gamble swallowed a dictionary when he was a boy," folklorist Thelma Boltin of Gainesville once explained.)

So emotionally caught up was Rogers in his act that he might have been a Southern preacher exhorting the flock to sin no more, but if you listened closely to his word pictures you began to see more. A sample: "Winding out of the Georgia Piedmont like a malignant magic carpet of concrete is Interstate Highway 75. It bores relentlessly southward, splits the sovereign beauty of Florida asunder. It passes the greatest commercial concession ever articulated in the entrepenurial visionings of modern mankind—a veritable monument to the legacy of Mickey Mouse—Disney World, a $500 million jukebox in the honky-tonk of life."

By then, it was clear: he was not John Brown at all. He was an imp poking fun at the curious weave in life that the special qualities of Florida made possible. He told of an encounter with a Georgia sheriff who wore a shoulder holster made of a sneaker with the toe cut out. He described the glory of a Lake George fisherman bouncing across the water in his boat at 83 miles per hour, sipping beer and "stirring a paper plate of potlikker and grits, nailed to the seat." He talked about a drunk who dynamited catfish, cut them into circular pieces, and sold them to tourists as scallops.

Gamble reveled in the absurdity of contrived lives in the natural paradise of Florida. His words caricatured Yankee tourists or newcomers as well as Crackers. Each recognized themselves in the mirror he held up, and enjoyed it. The process was healthy for all.

That was his act. In his rocking chair at home in St. Augustine, a two-story, shingled house that sat among trees and looked across Salt Run, a finger of the Matanzas Inlet, he reverted to being a man who liked to talk about the "psychic devices" people used to cover up their character. In my talks with him, he spoke of the "enigma of life" and his search for simplicity. He studied writers and philosophers. In particular, he liked William Faulkner.

"I read *The Sound and the Fury* three times before I even began to understand it," he once said. "I studied it, and it changed my life. I say that without qualification."

He also read James Agee, Thomas Wolfe, Eudora Welty, Carson McCullers, Harry Crews, pursuing understanding while enriching the depth, irony, and humor of his Southern folkloric stories and songs. He drew inspiration from the small pleasures and ground-level adventures of the ordinary Floridian.

Florida never had enough champions of that sort.

◊ Sometimes, the heroic side of miracle folk responded just before circumstance came crashing down. Bobby Howell was an example. When he was growing up, the Apalachicola river and bay were a certainty in his life. The river was sweet and clean. The bay was full of oysters. They would always be that way. They were bountiful and eternal. A Panhandle boy could romp and fish and do as he pleased, and nobody would suffer and nothing would become scarce. Ecology had not been discovered, or invented. As far as the environment was concerned, life was a fairy tale without a big bad wolf.

"You got to remember," Bobby Howell told me in 1982, "when we were boys we always heard that the river purified itself every seven feet. We all believed that."

So in the tight little town of Apalachicola, where five generations of his family had been born within the city limits, Howell did not worry. The river and the bay would take care of themselves. Even attending Florida State University, Howell still believed. He studied accounting and dwelled little on theory and life systems. Nothing shook his apathy. "I made a D in college biology," he said.

Yet, together, Howell and Franklin County became one of the dramatic stories of environmental awakening in Florida. The change came slowly. Not until he was forty-three years old did he realize that he should worry about the mighty river and the productive bay. By that time, Howell had become a powerful political figure in the county. From his grandfather, who had been county sheriff for 30 years, he inherited a taste for politics. In 1956, he ran for clerk of the circuit court and became the first clerk candidate to defeat an incumbent. By 1982, at age 53, he had won six straight elections. He had become a dapper, distinguished local politician as well as a brigadier general in the Florida National Guard.

Apalachicola, just 77 miles from Tallahassee, then was a Gulfside community with fine old Victorian homes as well as being the site each November of the Florida Seafood Festival, one of Florida's oldest celebrations. In those years it was a place that barely seemed to grow at all. In the 1930 census, it had a population of 3,143; in the 1980 census, it had 2,565. During that time, the county population increased by only 596 (to 7,661). Neither had the town changed in appearance much since he was a boy, Howell said. It had essentially the same storefronts, the same streets, the same families, nearly all of them involved in the $10 million a year local seafood industry, the same tightly controlled property.

"I can remember only three new buildings in downtown Apalachicola in my lifetime," Howell said then. "There was the bank and the clothing store behind the pharmacy, and the Ford Motor Co."

Howell said that about 10 years earlier he had become aware that growth was changing the rest of Florida. Particularly disturbing was the decline of state oyster beds. Pollution had spoiled so many of them that Apalachicola had been left as the producer of 85 percent of the state's oysters. The trend was upsetting. Most places had other industries if oyster beds closed, but Apalachicola had only seafood. Exploitive urbanization, spreading even toward Howell's quiet cranny of Florida, could damage both the pocketbook and the lifestyle of Apalachicola.

When marine biologist Dr. Robert J. (Skip) Livingston of Florida State University—a man who had miracle stature of his own—started his exhaustive studies of Apalachicola Bay, and began campaigning to save it from pollution, he recruited Howell as a bridge to local citizens. The goal was to protect the 107-mile length of the river in Florida, from Chattahoochee's Lake Seminole (formed in 1956 by the Woodruff Dam, which backed up the waters of the Flint and Chattahoochee rivers at the Georgia line) to the 212-square-mile Apalachicola Bay rimmed by barrier islands. These were inseparable, Livingston said. Later he would include the entire length of the river, from where it flowed out of the Georgia mountains, past Atlanta, all the way to Florida.

The river touched six Florida counties (all sympathetic to the campaign) and was 80 percent bounded by swamps and marshes. "These old country boys up here like to fish, too," Howell said.

The first major step in the campaign was to create the 192,758-acre Apalachicola River and Bay National Estuarine Sanctuary. In the political battle to win that federal designation, Livingston and Howell at one point flew to Washington, D.C., for a hearing. The night before the hearing, they sat around talking. Howell told Livingston some personal stories of what the river and the bay meant to the people of Franklin County.

Next day, Livingston had the entire program alone, or so Howell thought, but when Livingston stood up he turned it over to Howell. "Bobby," he said, "you take the first 30 minutes. Tell 'em what you told me last night."

Howell, trying to remember what it was he had said the night before, got up and articulated his gut feelings. His presentation was simple, practical, and compelling. As he talked, he convinced himself, too. That was the final step in the awakening of Bobby Howell. To protect themselves, Howell and Apalachicola learned that they had to protect the river and the bay. The sanctuary was established.

In Florida, such a fight never ends—hurricanes and urban pollution are unending threats to the oyster beds—but Apalachicola became one of Florida's clearest proofs that environmentalism carries a business payoff, and that citizens will defend their communities when they understand what is at stake.

Some miracle folk, like Faye Rains of Cedar Key, took on their status because of artistic skills.

The Gulf and salt marshes made an island of Cedar Key; you crossed four bridges to get there. It was a tight little fishing community that had endured historic hard luck—touched by war, hurricanes, and depressions—and still survived. An outsider, Cedar Key old-timers said, was anyone who lived on the mainland side of the No. 4 bridge.

I had a weakness for fried mullet, inherited from my mother, who understood that fresh mullet properly fried was a delicacy. I learned about it early. I made my first trip to Cedar Key at the age of two weeks. Nothing stirred old memories and made me wax more philosophical about the genuine things of Florida than mullet and grits for breakfast. Mullet had its own mystique in Florida. Elsewhere it was a trash fish. Even in Florida, for years it had been a bait fish except to fishermen and Florida insiders. There was a Cracker honesty about it and a distinctive taste that symbolized neglected Florida values. Crackers tended to like it. Mullet hunger involved a yearning for the beautifully rough edges of unhomogenized Florida.

In 1985, even in Cedar Key there was only one place to get that old-fashioned morning fare—the Rains Cafe, where tourists seldom trod. Out on the dock, there were three fine restaurants. In town, there were at least three more. Tourists loved them all, with good cause, but only Rains Cafe had fried mullet for breakfast, and for a while even Rains considered it a special offering.

The white frame, red-trim building with neon beer signs in the window sat by the third bridge, the one over a narrow stretch of water called The Canal. It sat across the street from a seafood market manned by local fishermen.

Old-time Cedar Key folk, many of them regulars, ate there. The place included a bar and a pool table and a clubby Cracker atmosphere that might be considered the Cedar Key version of *Cheers.* In 1985 if you went there late in the morning, Faye Rains, who had the weary look that all good and understanding women acquire, would recognize the symptoms. If she was having a good day, she would disrupt her small kitchen, overrule the protests of her assistants (in her small kitchen, scrambling eggs and frying mullet at the same time was a conflict of taste), and serve fried mullet to a stranger in need.

She would send someone across the street to get a couple of fresh mullet. She dressed and battered them, and soon a pair of golden brown mullet would arrive on a plate, accompanied by a deep dish of grits graced by a gob of butter the size of an egg yolk. For a mullet fancier, this was Buckingham Palace and, smiling by the hot stove, was Queen Faye.

Rains was born in Cedar Key. Her father, also born in Cedar Key, was a fisherman. Her husband, Al, an outlander born a few miles east on the Suwannee River, was a fisherman. Her son was a crabber. She grew up on mullet and grits. She ran the restaurant for two decades, cooking all her life for fishermen who were particular about how their fish are cooked. She had tested and experimented and improvised to find the best ways to batter and fry a mullet. She knew how.

"I learned it myself," she said one November morning in 1990, a time when the mullet were full of roe and in high season. "Kept mixing it up and frying it out until I got it the way I wanted it. Never wrote it down. Never had to. First thing you have to do, be sure you get fresh mullet."

At her place, you knew. No mullet ever grew old under the Rains roof. She stocked it plate by plate, order by order. Sometimes, your breakfast order might be briefly delayed while she sent across the street for more fresh fish. A waitress might have to wait while they were filleted. The ceremony and the wait enhanced the treat.

In the Rains kitchen, you were in the presence of a mullet master. For years, she did not serve it for breakfast except under special persuasion. Finally, though, the requests came too often. She gave in to public demand and revamped her facilities to create a mullet breakfast special—fried fillets, grits with that big old butter eye in the middle, and toast. Instead of using the grill, she deep-fried them. It guaranteed mullet eaters an everyday fix at breakfast. Fridays, there was a double mullet feature, not only breakfast but a luncheon offering of fried mullet, lima beans, grits, and cornbread. Friday was her busiest day of the week.

When she sprinkled cornmeal, flour, and assorted seasonings, they fell upon the fillets like stardust, magically transforming them. She slapped them into the grease in full view of all, where they sputtered and popped provocatively, and shortly she drew them out, golden brown and slightly curling at the tail, changed from things of poor reputation into food for philosophers. The way she did it, the streaky-colored mullet with its healthy oil-moist flesh fried better than any fish recently alive.

For me, the Rains setting was plain perfect—Formica-topped tables, salt shakers loaded with rice to assure free flow, breezy fans circulating the air, local paintings on the wall, the pop of beer bottles opening at the bar, the click of balls at the pool table. There was a kind of hard times yet romantic reality about it all. The place just fit mullet and memories.

In Florida, mullet appreciation by the public at large seemed to improve in direct proportion to the loss of other available fish species. When the uninitiated Floridian could not get pompano or red snapper or grouper, for example, he was more likely to be brave enough to give mullet a try.

To real experts, the tip-off on mullet was that nearly all other fish loved to eat it, testimony amounting to peer acclamation. Pelicans and porpoises and osprey loved it, too. Asians and Californians and Hawaiians loved mullet, their pressure on the market making it the most valuable but least celebrated fish in Florida.

The sad end of the story is that Faye Rains closed her restaurant and retired. Other Cedar Key restaurants picked up the slack and put mullet on the breakfast menu, but it was not quite the same. Finally the state put limits on netting, and mullet, of all things, became scarce. The likelihood of another Faye Rains coming along grew dim.

Colors came to the eye of James F. Hutchinson in ways that the rest of us didn't see until he painted them with the touch of an old master. Then they enlivened a canvas and enriched our perspective on the world. His work kept the disappearing beauties of natural Florida alive, but as those wonders dwindled in the real landscape, there were fewer and fewer who fully understood what true marvels his canvases were.

Under Hutchinson's brush, a summer storm moving across the Everglades became a classic event that suggested the subtle seasons and mysterious geography of South Florida. His expressive lines drawn on the somber face of a Seminole hinted at the dramas of a checkered Indian history and at stories only partially told. His rendering of a dune-rimmed savanna, where spatterdocks decorated shallow ponds, gave spectacular evidence of geologic evolution, the landscape-altering rise and fall of the ocean. Hutchinson paintings brought form and color to visionary truths about heritage.

Beginning at age eighteen, Hutchinson learned to make magic of the Florida realities, enhanced them, portrayed them at their Sunday best, laid them out proudly so that they could be better appreciated and understood. His body of work, exhibited and lauded widely in world's fairs and national tours and museums and universities, made him a Florida icon, a talent treasure. To me, he was a friend and simply the best at what he did.

For 24 years, he and wife, Joan, lived in a big-beamed barnlike house that fronted the Indian River near Stuart. Their sons, Kevin and Kelly, grew up there. The Hutchinsons woke up mornings to a sunrise that rose out of the ocean, moved across Hutchinson Island and the Indian River, and lit up the small patch of jungle that screened their world.

Their Florida was a jewel, the best of it in their eyes. In 1996, when he was 63, with mixed emotions but excitement about a challenging new passage in life, he and Joan sold their big house on the river and moved to a mountainside home on the island of Hawaii. Hutchinson was discouraged by the growth and development that was changing Florida. He needed to recharge. He wanted to study new colors and life forms, and paint them as he had Florida. He would continue to do Florida paintings, but from afar, from the perspective of memory and with the inspiration of new surroundings. He and Joan would come back periodically, if not permanently, to refresh their grasp and revive their old enthusiasms.

"Every decision I ever made was probably an emotional one," he once told me. It helped explain the later move to Hawaii.

His passion for art began as a teenager, probably inspired by the celebrated Florida landscape artist Beanie Backus, his brother-in-law. He never took lessons from Backus, but the artistic example was there. After 10 years of painting and working at odd jobs to keep the family going, he and Joan (they met as art students at Florida State University) took a gamble to establish his identity. Against the advice of Backus, they moved to the Seminole Indian Reservation at Brighton, northwest of Lake Okeechobee. There, grubbing for a living, scraping bugs out of his oils, they spent most of the next four years. Hutchinson—living among the scenes that became his brilliant trademark—learned to paint.

"Until then I was an amateur," he said.

The study of Indians and their place in history became another passion. Although he painted in Europe and Africa, Florida and Indian art—including Western Indians as well—became his specialities. In 1965, the state selected 35 of Hutchinson's Indian paintings for the Florida exhibit at the New York World's Fair. Many honors, and new identification as a serious artist, grew from that. During the 1970s he was commissioned to do 50 paintings for the University of Miami. It took him six years.

Joan and Jim long ago earned their place among the miracle folk. Hutchinson art defined the best of natural Florida and preserved it.

((In a lifetime of living in Florida and nearly a quarter century of professionally rambling the state, I found so many miracle folk that only a suggestion of their numbers can be made, only a sampling can be offered. Their names occur throughout these chapters. Some were put into an earlier book, *Becalmed in the Mullet Latitudes*. I did not always find them in the courthouses or the statehouses, or in the newspapers or on television, although sometimes I did.

((Elizabeth Smith lived in Crawfordville, the seat of Wakulla County, a short drive south of Tallahassee. With a schoolteacher's eye for the long view of history and a hand-cranked mimeograph machine, she created a publication during the 1960s and 1970s that reflected the daily lives in that then-underdeveloped county and gave them the dimension of folklore. Anyone interested in the real Florida was interested in the *Magnolia Monthly*, as she called it.

The *Magnolia Monthly*'s circulation hovered just under 300. It sold no ads, and a subscription cost six dollars a year. Still, the names on its subscriber list had addresses ranging from Alaska to New York to Miami. She managed to be a fresh and fair voice that was heard—liberal in many of her views, outspoken, and accepted. Her spicy comments and well-researched area histories made her an insider's favorite among Tallahassee politicians.

Of Reubin Askew, an outstanding governor, she once noted: "He was liberal enough for South Florida and pious enough for North Florida." Askew was the philosophical heir to the heroic former governor LeRoy Collins, a man who put conscience into his politics. For Smith, Askew was almost too good: "I'm suspicious of a man without any bad habits," she wrote.

When Elizabeth F. Smith lost her life to cancer in 1977, Florida lost one of its truest voices. In her last issue (April 1977), she announced her farewell with her usual clarity and simplicity, apologizing for the interruption of service and asking subscribers to tell her whether to refund the $3.60 left on annual subscriptions or give it to the American Cancer Society. "God bless you for your interest," she ended it.

John Pennekamp by nature and profession was a shy man of German ancestry who dealt in headlines, but few saw the shy side of him. In 1925 he followed his Cincinnati sweetheart, Irene Quillian, to Miami, then a city of 100,000, and went to work for *The Miami Herald.* She became his wife, and he became the hard-charging, blunt editorial voice of *The Herald.* Old-timers in Miami said that city politicians visited his office with their hats in their hands.

In his time Pennekamp was involved in, and sometimes directly responsible for, virtually every significant development in Dade County. However, he is principally remembered as a conservationist who played a critical part in establishing the Everglades National Park and the John Pennekamp Coral Reef Park at Key Largo.

Typically, he never thought of himself as a conservationist. Though he received many national and state awards for his conservation efforts, serving voluntarily as a consultant to federal agencies and on state commissions under five Florida governors, Pennekamp saw it differently. "I was a newspaperman, not a conservationist," he told me in 1974. "That got me involved in the parks system. I just got interested."

By the time Pennekamp became involved, the idea of an Everglades National Park was already a half-century old, principally fostered by Miamian Ernest F. Coe. In 1944, Governor Spessard L. Holland told John S. Knight, editor, publisher, and co-owner of *The Herald* (Pennekamp was titled associate editor) he thought the park could become a reality if Pennekamp got behind it. "Can you do it?" Knight asked Pennekamp. He could. "JSK put up the money and I went at it," Pennekamp said.

Florida's final step in raising the money necessary for its part in the project involved a poker game that elevated Pennekamp into Florida folklore. The state legislature then was ruled by rural legislators called the Pork Choppers (so dubbed by the *Tampa Tribune* because they fought for "pork, rather than principle"). Any funding would have to go through them. Friends helped Pennekamp make their social acquaintance, and he joined them in a poker game at Orange Springs in North Florida. After a Cracker dinner of fried chicken, collard greens, and cornbread, the group settled down to a nickel-and-dime game. Pennekamp, enjoying an extraordinary run of luck, won hand after hand.

One of the players, Pennekamp recalled, was Bill Pearce of Palatka, chairman of the Senate Finance Committee. After Pearce laid down what he thought was a winning hand, muttering about the Pennekamp luck, Pennekamp topped him with three kings. "Just how much money do you need for that goddam park of yours?" Pearce said. Pennekamp replied, "Two million dollars." Pearce responded with what proved to be a commitment: "Then why don't you come over to the legislature and get it instead of taking it out of our pockets."

The park got its state money. "That was the way with the Pork Choppers," Pennekamp said. "When they said something, that was it." President Harry Truman dedicated Everglades National Park in a speech at Everglades City in 1947.

The idea for a coral reef park in the Keys originated with a biological conference in 1957 that passed a resolution calling for the U.S. Department of the Interior to save the coral reefs. Pennekamp picked up the idea, gathered support, and pushed hard. At the park's dedication in 1963, Governor LeRoy Collins paid Pennekamp unusual tribute, calling him "the father of our great Everglades National Park," and adding: "There may be others who have loved Miami and Florida more but none have I known who has proved it through service more dedicated. We owe him— and future generations will always owe him—a great debt."

Pennekamp was flabbergasted that the park would be named for him, and he worried that it might upset the financing. "I didn't know a thing about it. I thought it was a mistake," he said. "I thought, 'Who the hell's Pennekamp? The legislature won't put up any money for it now'."

They did and he became one of the few miracle folk to enjoy such grand memorials. One other who did also got her start in the newspaper business.

❡ Tiny Marjory Stoneman Douglas badgered her way among the giants of industry and development like a fearless Lilliputian princess searching for truants among the Gullivers. She was a miracle even among miracle folk. Proceeding elegantly along in a floppy hat and a flowered dress, she kicked the behemoths in the shins if they erred, flatly scolded them if they acted without scanning the far horizon first, and managed in a deadly but ladylike way to alter the perception and sometimes the order of things for the better. She was a child of the Victorian period but a heroine for all times. I wrote about her often, but it never seemed enough.

From her height of five feet one inch, weighing less than 100 pounds, near blind, she nevertheless managed to make a microscopic study of the world through thick-lensed glasses, and she unfailingly considered herself a warrior. In 1984 she wrote me a letter, one of many such treasured messages. I had described her in a column as frail, and she did not like that. "Dearest Al," she wrote. She began with flattery and then added: "I am about as frail as a small, coarse horse. . . . With love and adulation, Marjory." That was Marjory, clear-eyed and direct about everything, including herself.

The older Marjory Stoneman Douglas got, the more celebrated she became, and that was impressive, for she was born in 1890 and was still going strong well past her hundredth birthday. Among the miracle folk, she was the grande dame. She was like the last panther—so different from the rest of us that she could be the last of a species.

Her vision of Florida, with a focus on the Everglades, always had the clarity and frankness of a wild thing. The most famous of her eight books, *The Everglades: River of Grass*, elevated the Everglades from a giant swamp into wetlands mythology, a place acclaimed for keeping South Florida from turning into a desert.

Once, an environmental group in the Keys accustomed to outlanders rhapsodizing about the memorable overseas drive to Key West was momentarily stunned by her. She noted the garishly tacky roadside gauntlet of commercialism that walled the drive and commented, "It's ugly, just ugly."

She spoke with a faint accent, almost British. "I studied elocution at Wellesley," she once explained, "and I've been going around elocuting ever since."

At another meeting where environmentalists were mulling over their problems, she stood up and shed blood. "Our problem is with the people who are only mad for money," she said. "They cannot be people that we respect very much. . . . These are not worthwhile people at all." She paused and turned impishly practical. "But if there are any of them here today, please see me at the end of the meeting."

Of John Pennekamp, hailed as the father of the Everglades and a man whom she admired, she once said, "I wouldn't call him the father, though. He was more like the midwife."

During a gathering at Art Marshall's North Florida enclave near Interlachen, in 1982, she further explained her view of early Everglades heroes. "Actually, I think the man who really thought it up was Harold Bailey, whom people might not remember at all. He was an ornithologist and lived in Coral Gables. All Harold Bailey did was take Ernest Coe [the landscape architect whose persistent crusading for the idea of an Everglades park was critical to its creation] out and give him a good look at the Everglades. Bailey never did any more than that, but that made a difference.

"Father [Frank B. Stoneman, who sold *The Miami Herald* to John S. and James L. Knight] gave Coe his first support. He wrote editorials for the park. Dear Mr. Coe was a terrible bore. When Ernest would come to the office, Father's heart would sink because he knew it would be an hour. Ernest would read him every letter he had ever written. He wanted the park to include a good deal of the Big Cypress and what later became the Pennekamp Park. He was right, but it couldn't be done at the time. Senator Holland and Ruth Bryan Owen had a great deal to do with pushing the park. She was William Jennings Bryan's daughter and the first woman Congressman from Florida." Mrs. Ruth Bryan Owen of Miami was elected in 1928 to represent Florida's Fourth Congressional District, then stretching on the east coast from Jacksonville to Key West and inland to Orlando. She served four years.

On one occasion, after Douglas urged that farming interests, especially sugar, be pushed out of the Everglades, a man of opposite view seethed. "What would you do for food if you got rid of all the farmers?" he asked. That drew a typically irreverent Douglas sidestep that only made the anger worse. "Open another Winn-Dixie," she said.

Douglas had an idea once that she wanted to replace the word *ecology* with something more understandable. "I've thought of a new word I'd like to use instead. I'd like to call it *geo-planning* (geology-geography). Until we come up with a better word, I'd like to use that. When they say *ecology* I'm never quite sure what they mean," she said.

She spent her late years with her nurse in her cottage at Coconut Grove near Miami. She listened to book cassettes, talked with friends, kept an eye on Florida. I last talked with her by telephone just before her 103rd birthday. "I'm not doing very well at the moment," she said, clearly implying she expected to be back in the battle soon. She had come to Miami in 1915, when it was a hamlet, to work for her father's newspaper. She had watched Miami grow into an international city. She did not recoil from the change; she flowed with it. Her splendid reaction: "It's been like going over Niagara Falls in a barrel."

❦ The story of the miracle folk, all of these and many more, continues. They leave a magnificent legacy of deed and thought and, above all, inspiring example.

Home, Sweet Melrose

Those folk lucky enough to live snuggled up to the heart of natural Florida, in such deliciously out-of-the-way places as Melrose, enjoy quiet pleasures and surprises. Life centers around home, yard, neighbors, church, and community. Any day, the breeze can flip over a small leaf and reveal new threads of life, or lightning can split a live oak and suggest astonishing dimensions of strength and endurance, or a sunrise can strike the clouds in a way never noticed before and reflect new colors on the lake, or a new critter can trot up and put an exotic accent on a familiar path, or a neighbor mellowed by natural surroundings can perform an act of kindness that somehow makes the whole world seem kind. As every- where, good and bad things happen, but a surprising number of them are good and they arrive as unexpected gifts.

Down by the lake, a few minutes before sundown, a flock of about 200 white ibises came racing over each evening, sleek and swift and flying low in a vee formation along an invisible interstate in the sky. We had to watch closely for them. They could surprise us. They barely skimmed the treeline on the other side of the lake and then they swooped close to the water, so that from afar we could not frame them against the horizon un-

til they came on us, right over the gazebo, their long curved bills and streamlined bodies spearing the air, as intent and anxious and determined as long-distance runners.

There never was enough time to count or to study. They simply flashed across, leaving us wondering, trying to remember all the details. With sunset colors enhancing our woodsy setting, all else seemed to stand back and hush for the ibises. All you could hear was the beat of their wings: muted sounds, hollow bones and feathers beating powerfully against the wind.

We never could get enough of this. Late each day, we would go to the gazebo and wait for them to come again. We sipped wine, crumbled bread to throw to the bream that swam close to shore. An instant before flyover, the little fish became agitated, scattering into the reeds to hide, and then the ibises would flash by, laying upon us a mysterious blessing.

Florida, in the most civilized and polite of its wild guises, behaves like that. It spreads a quiet scene of such purity and beauty that it requires religious similes for proper appreciation. At the other extreme, when a hurricane howls out of the ocean from the direction of Africa, it still holds true. It can be hell. Between, there is a magnificent stretch of the charming and the alarming.

Ibises commute, and for a few weeks in 1985 we were on their route. Early each morning we saw their rear view. As though headed to work, they winged their way in squadron fashion across our lake to a preserve of wilderness scrub not far away, where the low sandhills were spotted with sinkhole lakes, where there are swamp areas rich in tasty frogs and grasshoppers and such. In the evening, they returned along the skyway above our house to large, wet prairie lands fringed by hardwood hammocks a few miles on the other side.

Dr. John W. Hardy, an ornithologist at the University of Florida, said that ibises are not migrants but full-time residents of Florida and might easily fly 20 or 30 miles each day in search of food. Their appearance had a simple explanation, he said: they change routes periodically. It was not simple to us.

There are different chapels for religion, just as there are different religions, and a time and a place for each. Not all of them need stained-glass windows or lovingly worn altar rails or gleaming brass and candlelight to strengthen the sense of infinity that can exist even in a tiny place. Some of them have rough concrete floors, like our gazebo, or no floors at all, just

dirt like that along our lakeshore, clean dirt, as we see it, because it re-
peatedly has been washed by little breeze-made waves that soak it smooth
and leave it with the look of mottled beach sand.

In our gazebo chapel (at least we had the bread and the wine), services
were determined by the sun, a higher order than the diocese. We assembled
for the sunrise and we reassembled for the sunset, and the messages stirred
our minds with wonder and gratitude.

Maybe that, in our different kind of chapel, amounted to a different
kind of sermon or prayer. In our case we did not question or try too hard
to define, in fear that we might spoil it. The benefits were many. We got
glimpses, if we were alert enough and sensitive enough, of a wisdom that
swept over us as startlingly as those ibises and then, too, often vanished as
quickly. We never forgot the feeling even though we might forget the de-
tails.

Some might call it irregular, not entirely proper, that at sunset we
should convene at a gazebo and pretend it is a chapel, and that from a
flock of ibises we would draw a maverick sense of piety. We did it anyway,
with our own prayer: may the ibises fly again, may the feeling last.

For nine fine years, we had another special gift from the wild, a bird
friend called Biddy, a tall white egret that sauntered about our yard,
roosted upon our roof, joined us for twilight watching, and fed at our
back door. She adopted us in 1976 after being tossed a few small bream as
she inspected the shoreline down by our dock. She became a fixture at the
house, a missionary from the wild bringing us behavioral messages we
spent many an hour trying to decode.

Biddy stayed with us through most of the calendar. She sprouted beautiful nuptial feathers around Christmas and left us for a few weeks each
February on what we imagined to be maternity leave, but she always
came back. Her return would be an occasion for celebration.

One day we would be sitting there on the porch, worrying about starving Ethiopians or personal obesity, or something else that profound, and
there would be a flash of those great white wings. Biddy would sail gracefully down out of the sky and take up residence again. She put a refresh-
ing sense of wonder into our lives, as though a minor and perhaps mis-
chievous angel had chosen our home as hers. If she were wading along the
shore of the lake, looking for fresh bream among the reeds, she would
come at our call. If she were hungry, she went to the backdoor to be fed. If

no one was there, she would stalk around the house looking for us until she found someone, sometimes staring through an office window at me until she got my attention, or peering down off the roof into the bedroom or porch.

One of our unforgettable memories came during the winter of 1977, when it snowed lightly in Melrose. I opened the backdoor late one afternoon to check on Biddy, and there she stood with her head hunched into her beautiful white shoulders, tiny snowflakes softly patting her feathers and piling up around her black, three-toed feet. Her long neck stretched up, and the beady black eyes, slightly crossed, stared across that yellow beak in a silent but moving plea. Every beef kidney (when we ran out of bream, we fed her strips of beef kidney) in the house was hers.

Year after year, Biddy stayed with us, repeating her role as elegant mendicant for visitors. I wrote about her several times. She adjusted to changes in the house and yard and once even sauntered through an open door into the kitchen. Ornithologists explained that the American or common egret lives 20 to 25 years and that they sometimes imprint on certain places or people and forever after remember or respond to them. In other words, she adopted us.

Biddy was a friendly mystery from the wild that brought surprise and love and proportion into our lives. She had an air of confidence and well-being and grace, which she shared with us. Then, in 1985, she went away and did not come back.

Old age or an alligator might have gotten her. It had to be something of that dimension. Biddy, we are sure, never would have abandoned us. For years after, we looked for that swoop of lovely white wings and hoped that somehow she would find her way back to our house. When we lost Biddy we lost something valuable, we think.

There are plenty of things in life to generate exasperated puzzlement or that offer temptation to give up and treat the whole thing as a puzzle without solution. Less frequent are the nourishing examples like Biddy, which take the simple and the commonplace and turn them into wonders that remind us of life's balances. Things like these are the unexpected gifts we cherish.

❦ Not all the surprises of country life are so enchanting, of course. Some are philosophically unsettling, but that, too, can be good. One day a five-foot-long snake crawled up on the front porch, intent on eating a little rain frog perched there, which was unwisely croaking out a loud message that we interpreted as predicting rain. About that time my wife, Gloria, went outside to sweep the porch. Halfway through, she discovered the snake, one sweep away, and it scared hell out of her. It scared the poor snake (a harmless rat snake), too. Gloria came screaming back into the house, shivering, complaining that she had brushed against danger, close and personal, right there on her front porch.

That was a fine country moment, the kind that puts the world into perspective. Simple things briefly usurped control. Crime and bigotry and taxes and pollution and scary international politics were forgotten. Stumped-toe reality took over, driving out everything else, all posturing, all irrelevance. It turned out to be a fine day, because we had been gently reminded, without suffering a coup d'état, that life's daily assumptions often have the substance of fog.

Getting intimate with a snake guarantees a degree of terror. Once, from the comfort of our lakeside gazebo, we witnessed the humiliation of a proud man with just such an incident. One moment he was standing there in the lake like a lion, about chest deep, cooling himself. The next, he was bellowing operatically, creatively devising combinations of words that expressed great fear, but he did not move. No word exceeded five letters, unless you count hyphens.

He was a fellow whose nerves had been pre-steadied. On a hot summer day he had been sucking beer cans in the shade while his family swam in the lake. When the children came out, and the sun dropped low and the water grew still again, he strolled in and stood there for a moment, contemplating. About then, it happened.

As he explained later, he watched something shadowy swim out of the weeds, and he felt a long, cold snake coil around his left leg. Above the water, he strained to express pure panic; below the surface, so as not to rile the snake, he froze. Shortly, the snake unwound itself and swam on, harming no one. Pale, shaken, the man scampered out of the water and popped a fresh can of pacifier. It became our favorite snake story, a four-letter opera.

Presidents and prime ministers rarely have the benefit of such everyday experiences. Layers of bureaucrats and diplomats rob them of those humanizing little trivialities that remind us of frailty and nudge us back into practical focus. In small places like Melrose the folk have these things. We have time to be both foolish and wise, and we are.

Where we live, out in the woods six miles from unincorporated Melrose, on a map our place would be a tiny dot of green (live oaks, palms, pines, wax myrtles, magnolias, dogwoods) beside a clear lake. Here, we have learned anew that all life is a swap and a balance. You choose, and you pay local coin.

Wildlife crowds into our wooded six acres. Dead trees stand uncut, as gourmet encouragement to wildlife, providing bugs for food and cavities for nests or dens. Fences insure reasonable security. A good hunting season is when nothing gets killed. Alligators have crawled up on our beach with turtles in their jaws; deer have nibbled at our young trees; possums have burgled our dogs' food bowls; raccoons have ripped open our bird feeder; snakes have crawled into the azaleas by our bedroom windows and eaten songbirds from their nests; squirrels have gnawed holes in the pump-house door; eagles and hawks have dived on rabbits and other small game, and buzzards have circled over their leavings.

When the azaleas bloomed, carpenter bees swarmed around and even into our house, boring into the planking and making sawdust float down the sides of the house. Once a bee bored a neat, clean hole through the backdoor and came into the kitchen. Another spring when the bees came back, pileated woodpeckers—the huge ones that natives call the "Lord God" bird—came to our rescue. As bees attacked the dock and the carport, woodpeckers went after them. Splinters and chips flew.

During summer storms, we regularly have adventures with lightning. It has hit the tallest pine tree in our front yard and a magnificent live oak in the side yard, cutting a long gash down the trunk from limb to root and firing missiles of bark at the house, breaking windows. It knocked out our television satellite dish. It blacked out my computer. It exploded the wiring on a portable phone. It melted down the heat pump. We are not singularly cursed. A quarter mile away, a neighbor's kitchen appliances blew, and the kitchen caught fire. These are the usual summer occurrences. Even in our blessed little refuge, nature requires a tax. It is not so different anywhere else.

These lessen but do not eliminate the classic risks of complacency that legend says accompany life in small places. These have to be guarded against with the same care that New Yorkers and Miamians use in dealing with traffic and crime. The view from Melrose, and other small places, is like a peephole on the world. The angle is distant, as from the bleachers or maybe the end zone; the perspective is long and owlish, not mainstream.

Small-town folk who encounter skinned knuckles and stumped toes and an occasional snake on the porch (we still have porches), earn detachment that lets them look beyond snakes and frogs to worry about cities out of control, social divisions widening, public education in disarray, a range of businesses and institutions staggering. From afar, Melrosians have their own view of the world and it looks foggy out there; but those out there in it sometimes seem too busy to notice.

℣ For many city folk, who never met a salamander or dueled an armadillo or shared a newspaper with a squirrel or had a snake crawl out of the woodpile stacked neatly by the fireplace, country living offers escape—the illusion of order and serenity. Country makes them feel good, whether it changes anything or not. In their idle time, they *ape* (the verb is perfect) country folk. They patronize the country catalogs, read the country stories, wear country clothes, and listen to country music. They make an industry out of a masquerade. They envision the country life as a day camp for adults—permissive, supportive, nurturing. It is an education when they encounter *irruptions*.

Irruption is the phenomenon of sudden, puzzling animal behavior, like the compulsive march of lemmings to drown themselves in the sea. The term here is used within the context of our front yard, where the requirements of drama are less demanding.

Overnight, a mysterious and unseen creature had come out of the woods and begun to lay a pattern of small dirt piles across the yard, at the rate of one or two per day, eating a hopscotch path in the grass. It was an irruption. As long as the creature headed to the woods on the other side, it seemed sporting to let it eat and go its way in peace, but when it turned around and started back, the entire yard seemed in jeopardy. After a small tree began to tilt suspiciously, as though something underneath were tugging at its roots, it was time to call in the neighbors.

Country neighbors (anyone who lives within a mile or two) will do almost anything to help you, especially if they also can get a laugh out of it. Salted among the natives and old-timers are other neighbors who also came as refugees from the city, which is good: they arrived with illusions intact that in the country almost everyone is a good neighbor. Therefore, they helped make the illusions true.

On the scene of our mystery irruption, before helping out, these fine neighbors wanted to hear the details of the predicament. They wanted to savor and enjoy the situation, perhaps chuckle about it and tell you how it was in the old days when things were much worse but apparently a lot more fun. Since that was their only pay, it seemed reasonable.

Identification was the first problem. In Florida, there are armies of exotic little creatures that can alter your life, beings that city folk have not met personally. We explained the problem to the neighbors. They smiled and chewed over the details. You say this creature is tearing up your yard, eh? These little piles of sand came marching, did they? You raked them flat and they kept coming, eh? This was real country stuff. Soon the explanations came. It was an armadiillo, one declared. Another suggested squirrels. One chose fire ants. Mole crickets, another thought. One felt sure it was a salamander.

I always liked multiple-choice tests. If you do not know, you eliminate. I once had encountered an armadillo rooting in the yard, thumped it on the back with my walking cane, and it leaped straight up. Armadillos made a mess; they did not leave neat little sandpiles. This was not an armadillo.

I have had quarrels with squirrels, too. They bury acorns about the yard and then spend the rest of the year trying to remember where, digging small holes here and there in the search. I had been watching the squirrels. They were busy with other crimes.

The culprit was not fire ants, either, because there were no ants in the marching dirtpiles. It was not mole crickets, because I had observed their modest tunneling on the other side of the house, where they laid a three-dimensional stripe across the grass. This was different.

Therefore, it was a salamander. Trouble was, the encyclopedias said that what country folk called salamander actually was a small, ratlike pocket gopher with sharp teeth and long claws. The neighbors took the news very well. Over on Long Pond, the next lake, Mary Lou and John Swearingen (old-timers not fearful of such critters) trapped one and brought it to me as proof. "You're right," John said. "See?" They offered me my own dead pocket gopher, for which I thanked them but declined. Our neighbors will do anything for you. The irruption passed. Serenity was restored and our illusions about country neighbors strengthened. That is the country way.

❦ Small towns open up to you slowly. It takes years to know them. There is not the anonymity that city folk commonly suppose. Cities are long on numbers, short on memories; small towns are the opposite. What goes on in a small town? Small things go on. The tangle is not so different, but the focus is more human. Every event has a familiar face to soften harsh edges. Living takes up most of the time. Hardly anything else gets attention. While country folk might be hard put most of the time to meet the requirements for one good headline, they more easily set standards for a good life. The two ought not be confused.

Melrose, 65 miles southwest of Jacksonville and 20 miles east of Gainesville, was founded along the Bellamy Road (federally authorized in 1824, three years after Florida became a U.S. territory), which ran from St. Augustine to Tallahassee. The community took shape in the late 1870s as a winter refuge for Northerners. It grew up around Melrose Bay, which opened into the larger Lake Santa Fe. Melrose was about halfway between the coasts.

The Florida Railroad (from Fernandina Beach on the Atlantic Ocean to Cedar Key on the Gulf Coast), completed as far as Gainesville in 1858, came closest at Waldo, a few miles away by dirt road. Most visitors used that, but some reached Melrose by taking a boat down the St. Johns River out of Jacksonville to Green Cove Springs, traveling from there over dirt roads. (Later, a small railroad for a short time would link Melrose and Green Cove).

After the Civil War, with frontier Florida trying to encourage development, Melrose benefited. In 1877, announcement came that a canal would be cut linking Lake Santa Fe to other lakes and then to the railroad at Waldo. The same year, Melrose was platted and surveyed. In 1881, after completion of the canal, small steamboats carried passengers and freight across the lakes from Melrose Bay to Waldo. The *F. S. Lewis,* a 90-foot stern-wheeler, first made Melrose a water port.

Two books by Zonira Hunter Tolles of Melrose—*Bonnie Melrose* and

Shadows on the Sand —and *Yesterday in Florida* by Kennie L. Howard of Melrose, plus an *Architectural and Historical Survey* compiled by Murray D. Laurie tell the Melrose story. It is highlighted by a period in the late 1800s when Melrose flourished both as a winter resort and citrus center. (In the mid-1800s, the principal crop had been Sea Island cotton.) Growth slowed after the historic freezes of 1894–95 drove much of the citrus farther south, and as the Flagler and Plant hotel and railroad developments siphoned tourists and settlers and attention toward more easily accessible locations.

Ever after, Melrose was left with a touch of ambivalence about the whims of history. Some, preoccupied with business profits and the difficult processes of making a living, lamented that the growth whirlwind went elsewhere; others, thankful for a quiet life, feeling blessed that the lakes remained attractive and large patches of natural scenery graced their surroundings, rejoiced that it did.

For Miami migrants like us, grown weary from trying to break into chain-link traffic, longing to tread paths again that would accept footprints, not satisfied by static concrete shade that (unlike leafy shade) doesn't jiggle and dance in the breezes, life in Melrose was different. Within a 25-mile radius, there were an estimated 50 lakes—some as clear as springs, some as dark as strong tea because of the cypresses lining their shores, some (like ours) small and relatively private, others (like sevenmile-long Lake Santa Fe) large enough for major recreational activity. The lakes scattered great contrast across the scrub environment, the surrounding small farms, and the pecan groves.

In two hours or less, you could drive west to Cedar Key on the Gulf; or, if you preferred, you could drive the same distance east to St. Augustine and the Atlantic. The Suwannee, Santa Fe, and Ichetucknee rivers flowed within easy reach north or west; the St. Johns River curled its northward path 30 minutes away to the east. Like a beacon, shedding enlightenment in all directions, the University of Florida anchored nearby Gainesville.

Yet, out where we lived, it remained charmingly rural. If night in the city fell as blackly as it did around our house, with so few lights in sight, there might be a panic. In the country it enhanced the scene, for night was a time to sleep, and the dark accented the sunrise and the sunset. When the flowers bloomed, we smelled them. When the fruit on Felicity Trueblood's and Jim Dennis's U-pick-'em muscadine vineyards ripened in August, the Melrose grapevine (appropriately) spread the word. When the manure piled up in the pastures, we knew that, too.

We enjoyed small mysteries. One year, an area garbage collection box, one of the big green Dumpsters, disappeared. State beverage agents found it in the woods, full of mash. Welding alterations and a butane-gas cooker had converted it into a 500-gallon moonshine still. Over the years, the world intruded on our tranquil landscape: a small plane crashed in the woods, a couple of marijuana busts occurred, at least two murders were associated with the area, a nudist camp lasted on the prairie one year until winter came, a couple of houses burned, lake levels rose and fell with good rain years or droughts.

When we moved into our lake house in 1974, you reached it by three miles of dirt road, a daily adventure. Around the lake we had two houses occupied full-time. Urban Florida reached in toward us. Within five years the road was paved and the number of occupied houses jumped to 15. A giant subdivision appeared, backing up to a neighboring lake. Nearby, a 9,000-acre wilderness preserve took shape, providing housing for many rattlesnakes and coral snakes and gopher tortoises and used by the University of Florida to study the scrub environment. All that, plus an 800-acre Boy Scout camp across the road, saved the rural ambience.

For the first couple of years, we saw only strangers speeding down the two-rut road by our fence, heads bent over the steering wheel. In time, that changed. They turned into neighbors. We met some at the roadside mailbox, some at church; some came to the house with greetings and invitations and gifts of vegetables and firewood, or offers of neighborly help with common problems. Soon, out there in the woods a fine community of genial folk emerged—the Bishop clan (including the Swearingens and Shirley Lazonby) presided over by matriarch Millie, Peg and Ralph King, the Alsobrooks, Amber and Martha Wall, Reda and Don Williams, the three-branch Simpson clan, the Grants, the Barcos, and more. Others, like the Huletts and the McDowalls and the Traceys, stayed until age or deaths in the family forced them away. We learned to keep a loose hand on the wheel when we drove the six miles into downtown Melrose, because almost everybody waved and it was important that we wave back. It was identification. Outlanders did not wave back. The wave was a sign of fraternity.

Chiappini's general store and service station ("since 1935") at the crossroads of state roads 21 and 26 (a traffic light was installed in 1987) commercially anchored downtown Melrose, whose loosely defined borders touched four counties and where the population dispersed along the lakeshores and out into the woods. Four generations of the Chiappinis have worked at the store. David, born in the late 1940s, was running it as we were getting to know Melrose. Over the years, he and his wife, Marilyn, told us the story of the Chiappinis.

Dave's grandfather Joseph (Papa Joe) left northern Italy at age 14 with his father to help build the Holland Tunnel in New York. Before his work permit ran out, forcing him to return to Italy, he met a New Yorker named Lee Pearsall. Three years later, Pearsall sponsored young Joe's return to the United States. This time he stayed and became a U. S. citizen. Pearsall, who had a winter residence in Melrose, gave Joe a job there as caretaker. During the Depression, Pearsall paid Joe with gifts of land, including some at the Melrose crossroads. In 1935, with his $500 government bonus for having served with the U.S. Army in World War I plus a loan from Gulf Oil Company, Papa Joe opened the service station and general store. It evolved into an institution famed for its ready help and expert local counsel. It became a landmark and symbol, unofficially the capitol of Melrose.

Some now call Melrose the "Land of the Chiappinis." The family members are everywhere. All of Papa Joe's six sons worked at the store at one time or another. Ownership passed from Papa Joe to sons Francis and Maurice, and from them to Francis's sons, first to Dave (he later opened Chiappini Farm, a wholesale nursery business) and then to Mark and Robin. Dave's son, Andrew, has worked there off and on.

Andrew, a third-generation native of Melrose, was as protective of the area as his grandpa Francis had been. It was part of growing up and learning about Chiappini territory from a family that appreciated it, and then seeing it change in unsettling ways.

One hot day Andrew took a tractor out to mow underbrush along the edge of the woods. Debris was flying. The tractor hit something and flushed two deer—a doe and a fawn. The doe ran. Andrew, then 19, thought he had killed the fawn, but it struggled up—"bawling like a goat," he said, kicking at him. He held the trembling creature and smoothed its fur. The doe ran to the edge of the clearing, looked back, and pondered the situation a moment, then ran off again.

"It was a pretty little thing," Andrew said of the fawn, sounding a bit like a grown-up Jody, the boy in *The Yearling*. He held it for a few minutes, calming it, picking off ticks that had burrowed into its hide, brushing off the trash. Then he shooed it into the woods, where it ran looking for its mother.

Andrew had read the Marjorie Kinnan Rawlings book about a boy and a fawn growing up. He had seen the movies. He has visited the Rawlings home at Cross Creek. The story was familiar to him and all his friends. Rawlings's work was a real and alive presence in the area. He would have liked to keep the fawn, make it a pet, but he knew he couldn't. Not only did he have Jody's tragic example, but the law forbade it.

"You can't keep 'em," Andrew said, and related stories about others' attempts that led to bad results. In the book, Jody's deer ate the seed corn. In Andrew's experience, pet deer had gone berserk during rutting season, injuring keepers. One well-meaning woman kept an injured fawn until it got well, and then she let it go, but by then it was too late. It was no longer equipped for the wild. Dogs ran it down and killed it.

In North Central Florida, Rawlings did more than sell a lot of books and win a Pulitzer Prize. She imprinted the mythology of the region, the geographical equivalent of soul, and the imprint spun off into life after life after life.

The Chiappini store, a favorite with both locals and visiting fishermen (even journalists, who could sit at the small bar and drink beer while perusing the Melrose scene), sells everything from Dom Perignon champagne to earthworms for fishbait. For three generations now, it has provided sacramental wine to the local Trinity Episcopal Church. Francis, a kind and gentle man, ushered at early Episciopal services each Sunday until illness shortened his time. An Episcopal priest who married into the family conducts Chiappini christenings. On all things pertaining to Melrose, the Chiappinis have a reputation for caring and helping.

The Chiappini store sits diagonally across the intersection from Melrose Elementary School, where native Melrosian Donald Williams as principal shepherded the Melrose human future with such skill and care that most considered it his school in everything but name. In later years, a convenience store opened next door to Williamson's Grocery Store at the crossroads, joining the small crowd of buildings that now makes up downtown Melrose.

A one-square-mile historic district of fine old homes, many of them on Melrose Bay, was added to the National Register of Historic Places in 1990, thanks to the work of Historic Melrose, Inc. Beyond that, the fabric of Melrose includes small farms, churches, a post office, a fine little library (founded in the back of the Episcopal church around the turn of the century following a gift of books from the Society for the Propagation of Christian Knowledge in England), two banks, the phone company, a volunteer fire department, a cemetery, a few small businesses including Anne Lowry's antique shop, the Melrose Woman's Club, which hosted a historic marker hailing its building as the oldest (1893) woman's clubhouse still in use in Florida, and, depending upon the business cycle, three to four restaurants. Melrose Cafe earned a place as the designated weekend breakfast place; locals favored Blue Water Bay for dinner.

We attended a tiny church that was insignificant in almost every material way I can think of, but large in nearly all the others. Local carpenters built Trinity Episcopal, Melrose, in 1885–86 with lumber sawed from area trees. They formed the bricks in its pillars and fireplace (now removed) from local clay and left the interior plain and unfinished. To Trinity's credit, it honored the history and left the building largely as it was, almost museumlike. We sat on pews where the original half-dozen members sat, and the priest's words echoed off the same lovely, dark walls that were there in 1885 (the year that Sitting Bull surrendered to U.S. forces out West).

The old shingled roof was replaced with tin, and in church we could hear an oak leaf drop or the rain start. At the early morning service, which we favored, we easily could count the heads—good crowd (40) or poor (20)—and note their condition, along with everything else. On any given Sunday, we might note: Maureen Paul looks nice today in her big bonnet. Lay reader Charles Norton seems a little tired; maybe his back is hurting again. The wine from Chiappinni's store was tasty. Suki Hoffman scared us by tripping over the hem in her choir robe. Kathi Warren had a new outfit on. Pretty Kelly Brown and handsome Gram Alsobrook were growing out of their accolyte duties. Debbie and Mark Brown's other girls, Bonnie and Cristina, plus Gram's sister, Marion, and the Stegall children stood ready to take over.

At the front door, the aged or physically challenged leaned on handrails that were designed and installed by retired engineer Bob Simkins. Phil Thomson pushed his wife, Edith's, wheelchair up a side ramp also designed by Simkins. Volunteer ushers Carlton Paul or Larry Alsobrook (all the Alsobrooks officiated; Laurie the mother sang in the choir) or Mike Kreshka or Bob Van Giesen or Hank Chaires solemnly passed the plate. Tom Allensworth, the treasurer, stood ready to check the receipts. The Giesels, the Rynds, the Masons, and the Rices sang heartily and all "passed the peace" vigorously. Roll call was hardly necessary. We didn't often miss anybody, not sweet Roberta Gano smiling over in the corner with husband Ovid Gano or quiet Ruth Hulett, or regulars Edna Spratt, Peg Renzelman, Pat Poppell, and Esther Slazor.

After church, everyone gathered around the front steps, confirming those in-service observations, pontificating on the weather and catching up on the other news. If Yeltsin was in trouble and there was murder and rape in the Balkans, if somewhat bewildering criminality was taking place in Texas behind a religious shield, we put it aside for an hour or two of church-umbrellaed group therapy. We worried about more manageable things such as meeting the budget and keeping the lawn mowed, and we went back home in an elevated frame of mind. Pat Bonsteel and Liz Middleton would tell you that.

If you never have attended church in a small town, you have missed one of life's great quieter adventures. During one service, at a point when the Reverend Dale Warner thought he was delivering a rousing sermon about God intervening in human history, he paused in midsentence. People in the pews had begun ducking and dodging, flailing at the air. As he put it later, recalling an old song, "It reminded me of the Great Mississippi Squirrel Hunt."

It started when Bernie Gibbs, sitting one pew behind Lempi Warner, spotted a wasp on her shoulder, crawling ominously toward the bare skin of her neck. He swatted it off, giving Lempi a vigorous thump in the process. Then he reached to pick it up and got stung on his fingers, causing him to wring his hands and stifle a moan. The wasp fell in the aisle. He stood up and stepped on it triumphantly.

Wasps, nesting in the old church on and off for decades, had attacked mid-sermon. Neighborly parishioners waved roundhouse punches, slapped backs, crouched low, stomped the floor like flamenco dancers. The choir sang a little faster. When it was all over, a half-dozen wasps lay dead. The congregation was exhilarated, if a bit fearful. Gentlefolks Jean and Terry Marshall and Helyn Adkins would greet such a scene with widened eyes. Father Dale noted that never before had he had such an activist audience.

In a small church, these things happen. After another "storm of the century" had brushed through the area and many were left without power and water, Father Dale had a luncheon at his home. He called beforehand with the kind of sincere welcome joined to practical advice that you seldom can get from large institutions. "Go to the bathroom before you come," he said. The lunch was on, no matter what, but the storm had left the facilities unworkable.

This kind of thing helps make a man contemplative in church on Sundays, bending him toward the sunlight rather than the winter of the human soul. There might be a thousand small churches like Trinity in Florida, each doing their thing much the same way, but we in Melrose never thought so.

  Of all things, though, probably nothing put the heartbeat into our lives more symbolically than the old pendulum clock that sat in the living room, ticking away the minutes, chiming every half hour to remind us that time never stands still and neither can we.

My great-grandparents gave the clock to my grandparents on their wedding day in 1896. For the Burt family ever since, it has marked the rhythm of life like a metronome. The clock, 22 inches high and framed with oak wood, sat for about three quarters of a century on a mantle above a fireplace in what had been my grandparents' bedroom.

In all, six generations of Burts have listened to that clock. It has ticked and chimed from 1896 to now, overseeing the growth of the family tree, first the births of nine children and then the branching out of their children, the funerals of some. Many generations of Burts went to sleep listening to the clock, were called to the dinner table by it, lived by it.

We became caretakers of this family symbol (and the third owners of the clock) in 1989, when we inherited it from my parents. Again it sat in a kingly manner, positioned in a room with a fireplace. Though its sound competed with the others that we hear regularly by the lake—wind that drags leaves and twigs across the roof, birds that always find something to sing about, dogs (Lady and Brownie) that bark each time a squirrel dares to twitch or a deer strolls into the yard to eat corn at the feeder—it can be heard in every room of the house.

We became especially attuned to it, of course, and maybe that explains why it managed a quiet domination of the household—suggesting identity, offering inspiration, imparting larger purpose without intruding on the daily chores, managing to argue for discipline without imposing stress.

The swinging cast-metal pendulum, once gilded but now shadowed with wear, conferred upon each second a singular dignity, honoring it with an individual tick, and so accorded time the accurate perspective of elusiveness, importance, and inevitability. The chiming added definition to time. A single, resonant bong signals the half-hour, but on the hour itself the clock deliberately strikes the full count. Noon and midnight amount to minor celebrations.

The chiming has a musically declarative quality, not quite melodic but much more than merely percussive. For me, it is the sound of family, steadying, reassuring, comforting, while reminding that certain standards are expected and probably not being met.

To us the clock is priceless, but we doubt that it would impress anyone else very much. We have inspected it carefully. The woodwork has a good but homemade quality about it. The glass door bears a gilded pattern, somewhat faded, that depicts a bird and flowers while framing the pendulum.

The face of the clock, with Roman numerals, bears the initials "WC," and a small inscription on the rim reveals the clock to have been made by the Waterbury Clock Compamy in Waterbury, Connecticutt. Two worn keyholes on the face, where the springs for the chime and the pendulum are wound, affirm the clock's age. Lacquered labels on the back of the wood frame, some of the writing scratched off, advise that this is an eight-day, spring, striking clock and they offer winding and operating instructions. The clock fits our house.

When James Victor Andrew and his wife, Susan, gave their daughter Minnie and her new husband, 20-year-old Eddie Parks Burt, this clock in 1896 and sent them away on a honeymoon to Tennessee, which included a stay in the Alvin Hotel, they could not have imagined how it would keep time for so long and for so many.

They could not have anticipated that the second son deriving from this union would be named Alvin Victor, in memory of that nice honeymoon hotel and in honor of Minnie's father who bought them the clock. They could not have guessed that the clock would preside with such priestly presence for so long over so much quality family life, over so many fires and naps and chuckles and arguments and prayers. They could not have suspected that its chimes would call such an unending string of Burts to the dinner table, or that its gentle tick and toll one day would communicate a lot more than just the time.

Neither could they have foreseen that the clock would travel from a remote Georgia farmhouse in the foothills of the mountains to a city and then back to another remote house by the side of a clear Florida lake, the home of Alvin Victor, Jr., where it would be more prized than at any time since 1896.

Susan and James Victor Andrew, we suppose, would be pleased if they could know that their wedding present to Minnie and Eddie took on such stature in the family, and that it would tick out the rest of the 19th century and nearly all of the 20th and have an excellent chance to chime in the 21st—all while still in the hands of a Burt.

When the old Waterbury clock ticks and chimes, we hear many things, and they reinforce us. Sure, it is just an old clock, but the sound is special. It has six generations of family echoes, and they gave our little lake house the proper echoes and dimensions of home, sweet Melrose.

The Way of Florida

In Florida the future relies on the uncertainties of weather and the unknown mettle of arriving strangers. It makes an interesting life. Floridians have to learn to thrive on mobility and change, the ingredients of impermanence, and try to mold them into a sense of permanence. The state has tidal rhythms that affect all. To endure, we have to be flexible enough to bend but principled enough to hold on.

Florida seems forever poised on the edge of some new turn of an old cycle, some new migration that repeats history, or some impending natural phenomenon whose threat seems fresh only because it arrives to a new day and new conditions. Maybe nature remains comfortable with the erratic cycles, but the rest of us tend to fret and chafe at least some of the time—alternately drying out and parching under an extraordinarily close sun, becoming sopping wet from flooding rains, being pestered by mildew that creeps into the closets and clusters on our shoes and clothing. We enjoy no predictable constancy that permits us to perfect either our rain prayers or our sun worship. To love Florida, you have to love its contradictions and its exasperating extremes as well as its breathtaking beauty, its warm winters, and its natural inclination toward ease.

Life in Florida rides a pendulum from the sublime to the tacky and back, from serenity to unending traffic honks, from near tropical to temperate. All of it insures havens for abundant human variety, for many small and large surprises, for grounding grit and grunt among soaring marvels. Maybe nobody really understands Florida, except for a piece of it here and there for a brief time. Knowing that is a beginning. We build those sand castles and rebuild them time after time.

℘ Population pumps in and out, the totals ever rising. In the old days, population followed transportation. Ships delivered the newcomers at oceanports, boats carried them along the rivers. Then the railroads came along and extended the land reach. During my time, interstate highways laid down a major new dimension of access. Migration filled up South Florida first, spreading out from Miami and Fort Lauderdale and West Palm Beach, leaving a hole for the Everglades. I-95 from Jacksonville on down filled the gaps along the east coast. I-75 did the same toward the west, easily linking up the giant Tampa Bay metropolis—the state's new center of influence—with cities south and north. Alligator Alley connectors joined I-75 to I-95 in the south and I-4 began to put a linear city across the state from Tampa to Orlando to Daytona Beach. East-west I-10 brought Jacksonville, Tallahassee, and Pensacola closer together. The making of megastate Florida became a dream for real-estate salesmen and for any who felt that the best things in life could be measured by numbers.

In 1950, the population hit 2.8 million; in 1970, 6.8 million; in 1996, it was estimated at more than 14 million. During the 1980s, Florida received a net gain of 892 persons per day (using the out-migration formula devised by the University of Florida—for each two who came, one left—1,784 new residents arrived each day and half that number left). At their peak, the figures showed a movement of 2,000 residents per day.

If 2,000 alligators had crawled across the Georgia border every day looking for mud holes in Florida's diminishing swamps, there would have been panic. The governor might have called out the National Guard. If 2,000 fire engines had rolled into Florida every day, gleaming in the sun and looking for parking places, the legislature might have gone into special session. More quietly dramatic things than those happened every day in Florida for a quarter century, but we became numb to them. Mass movements were as regular as grocery shopping on Fridays. Ordinary folk invaded Florida, good and bad, rich and poor, skilled and unskilled, even like you and me, and they blended in. Few noticed their demands until the problems started popping up. In terms of uprooting lives, in terms of ambience lost, in terms of creating a transient atmosphere where diffusion of civic responsibility and accumulation of stress warped values and behavior, they made a significant difference.

In a state concerned about its water supply, for example, during the 1980s the U.S. Bureau of the Census said those 892 new residents arriving each day brought a need for 156,000 more gallons of fresh water every day. Living needs jumped dramatically—for electrical power, for police protection, for highways, for schools, for sewage disposal. Though they sliced across every aspect of life, their impact sneaked up on us. The numbers made us numb. They lost meaning. They afflicted us with population hypnosis, a complacent belief that tomorrow's numbers would pay for the problems created by today's numbers, and that rising numbers never would stop.

New Floridians made the state better in many ways, especially in the eyes of Midwesterners or Easterners not bred to the natural wonders of this state. They fueled the business community and gave the state a new diversity that allowed it to shed old ignorance and prejudice. They broadened horizons, paved a lot of roads, got rid of a lot of outhouses, killed a lot of mosquitoes, took on air-conditioning as a kind of religion. They made Florida a megastate with new political clout. Still, reaffirming the classic dilemma with nearly all progress, there was a swap.

Nobody would want to give up those things, but never have I felt that they should be paid for by cannibalizing natural Florida, by losing our sense of what Florida is and should be. It seemed too high a price, to me, that we should in effect have to disown who we are and what we are. I never felt we should have to turn our state into a facade of some other place, or that we had to mimic the manners and customs of some other region to bring in electricity and running water and modern government. I never felt Florida should have to give up its sense of place and identity to have paved roads and indoor plumbing. The issue is subjective: more a matter of values and standards that affect lifestyle, that affect the things that make life meaningful and rewarding.

Communities need soul as well as muscles. We have discovered, I think, the Florida principle of growth—that a place grows as long as it is attractive and stops growing when it becomes ugly. Business sense demands that Florida advocate laws and behavioral customs that keep the quality in our lives, so that in the long range we may have enduringly attractive and economically sound communities. The alternative is ugly communities with a future of declining business potential.

Growth management as a strategy arose because the state properly decided that growth should not inevitably mean a threat to quality of life. John DeGrove, a fourth generation Cracker and one of the miracle folk, became the guru of that tack. He introduced strategies of quality growth to Florida during the 1980s as head of Florida's Department of Community Affairs, appointed by Governor Bob Graham. DeGrove argued that there were no popular solutions for Florida's flash-flood population growth; any answer would seem imperfect but one had to be tried. He estimated in 1983 that new growth in Florida paid for less than 60 percent of what it required in public services, meaning that for years Florida residents had been paying 40 percent or more of the cost of public services for newcomers. He said growth should be managed, not fought. He had a vision to reshape the state, make it more focused, more orderly. He wanted future growth to be compacted within designated urban boundaries, and he wanted statewide standards for local taxes.

DeGrove had been a leader in the 1970s struggles under Governor Reubin Askew that sensitized Florida to its environmental jeopardy. He had spent ten years studying growth-management strategies in seven other states and had produced a major book, *Land, Growth, and Politics.* Governor Graham drafted him out of his job as director of the Joint Center for Environmental and Urban problems at Florida Atlantic and Florida International universities. If his efforts fell short of the near revolution in planning that he advocated, they nevertheless bent Florida in better directions. Growth management became a reality, if a hotly debated one.

Aside from being nettled by new regulations of any kind, some builders and developers also argued that growth management pushed costs higher and slowed growth. An answer to that came from county officials such as Maggy Hurchalla of Stuart (Martin County). "Every time we passed a growth-restrictive ordinance, somebody warned us we were driving away business," she told me in 1984. "But as a matter of fact, Martin County has grown faster and faster the more we've restricted it. The process only makes it a better place to live." Hurchalla, then a Martin County commissioner, was a member of the talented family of Renos in Miami, miracle folk all, three generations of whom had worked at *The Miami Herald*. Her mother, Jane Wood, had been a distinguished reporter for *The Miami News*. Her sister, Janet Reno, later became U.S. attorney general.

Whatever happened politically, an odd sensation spread among the folk of Florida with whom I talked, a kind of homesickness—a homesickness for the Florida that was slipping away from them. Floridians were getting homesick without ever leaving home. Homesickness took on the aura of exile.

Homesick seems an inadequate word to describe a condition of such emotional longing for home that even the things you complained about while there become highly appealing because you are not. There have been times, after long trips to faraway places, when little patches of familiarity among the strange would remind me of the pedestrian things of home, and the urge to experience them suddenly became almost a compulsion. That's homesick. Sometimes, it could be triggered by the slightly uncomfortable fit of a motel recliner, sometimes a warm glass of milk in a restaurant or a suspicious-looking hamburger. In response, I would be homesick for the rump-sprung chair back home, for fresh milk poured by chilled hands at the refrigerator door, for the smell of smoke from the backdoor grill, and the taste of a hamburger whose ingredients and construction I knew personally.

Little things did it as well as big ones. Now and then, for example, the urge seizes me and I need seafood, out of Florida waters, cooked as Floridians cook it. I get homesick for real Florida seafood, the soul fuel of the Florida fatherland—a pompano or yellowtail broiled in lime sauce, a fresh mullet fried in peppery, thin batter, a grouper or a snapper grilled over hickory chips. These are among the genuine things of Florida for which we can be thankful. Throw in oysters, shrimp, lobsters, and stone crabs, and visions of old-time Florida engulf you: beach campfires, swimming in breathlessly beautiful springs bubbling with water clearer and tastier than comes out of the faucet now, hiking through tall forests where the loudest sounds were made by the wind and the birds. The appetite for seafood represented the need to see, feel, smell, and taste the fundamental produce of Florida. For some of us, unpasteurized, unhomogenized, unprocessed Florida comes with scales and fins and gills, or shells and claws and tails. Ingestion of it revives a declining sense that this spectacular place has a rough-edged side beyond the influence of the tour-and-conquer set. Nothing else pacifies. Only Florida seafood pulls the trigger.

So it is disappointing, homesick-inducing, to visit a restaurant to get a Florida seafood fix and find that the only choices are mahi, tilapia, pollack, and catfish. The catfish are fine. They might have been raised in a Florida farmer's pond. The others (even though tilapia, too, is farmgrown) come across more like imports and pretenders, not exact fits for real Florida appetites.

Once, you could find all that wondrous Florida seafood almost anywhere, even at roadside stands. Now, you find it just here and there, usually near where the fishermen live, but sometimes you cannot find it at all. Recreational fishermen blame scarcities on the commercial fishermen, and the commercial fishermen blame it on careless coastal development and pollution. Whatever, the seafood disappeared and with it access to a valued trapping of Florida lifestyle.

One day we might say to the young Floridians, "Back in the old days we ate fresh ocean-caught Florida fish whenever we wanted," and they probably will doubt the veracity of such outlandish boasts. In the same vein, for perspective, we might also tell them that we drove Model T's and Model A's. We might stray afield and become even more suspect by declaring that in our time a breach of civility and courtesy in public places was an uncommon disgrace. Can you imagine?

The seafood dilemmas are modern. Any answers come at great wrench or hurt to someone, but there are answers: limited fishing seasons and techniques, tighter laws on coastal development (including rollbacks), stricter pollution controls, the immediate answer of more policing and the long-distance answer of more focussed education. Such Model T generalities and fair-share answers anger interested parties and terrify politicians, for few believe anymore that anyone will be satisfied with only a fair share.

So some of us get homesick about a range of things, even the offseason. Summer used to be the time of the year that Florida relaxed a bit, geared down after the busy tourist season. Crowds thinned and the traffic eased along the interstates, and all of Florida's lovely, identifying imperfections crept out in bolder relief. As the heat stirred and summer thundershowers threatened, as the mosquitoes began tuning their night songs that the tourists hate, it was a time of release and relief. A dedicated Floridian could search out sheltered places and comfortably commune with whatever side of the state he chose, ranging in sweep from favorite nooks in the buzzing cities to the sweep and silence of the swamps.

That changed. Now the season never really ends, for which the service industries at least are grateful, and the rules of survival never really stop changing. In the city a wrong turn off the interstate can be more dangerous than a wild gator, and maps do not indicate these wrong turns. The traffic roar never eases, not much. It is increasingly harder to find a quiet place that is neither a museumlike refuge with posted rules nor the subject of an environmental controversy and therefore not truly quiet. Any suburban lake might hold a gator, made dangerous rather than just cranky because it has to share habitat with people. Those imperfections that gave Florida summertime distinction, a little quiet time, and for which we old-timers acquired a loving taste, have been gelded by air-conditioning and concrete grooming. Parts of Florida, year-round, have taken on the disjointed feel of a mislocated franchise.

All that makes many Floridians, including me, homesick for the truth and beauty of home. If I had amnesia, no memories, maybe it would be exciting. As it is, it only makes me homesick. Across Florida there is the mark of economic cannibalism, a kind of self-predation that shouts doubt about the reckonings of tomorrow.

In a single year the different pieces of the state changed at different paces, so that in sum Florida seemed less to evolve than to warp into something new. Florida did not age as I expected, gradually and uniformly altering and maturing in predictable ways. Instead, it bulged this way and that, on the whims of migrating strangers and the eclectic demands of the various markets, as though some genetic tinkering might have been going on, producing new parts and a new identity rather than maturing an old one. So sometimes I felt like a homing pigeon who never flew away but suddenly could not with certainty identify the loved landmarks of home. The scene changed wrenchingly.

The homesick ones live among glimpses and impressions that remind them of loss. They have to develop a mindset that lets them see a sundown over the sawgrass or a flight of ibises over a lake and smile for what is there, not mourn for what was there. For old-timers it is not easy but homesickness should be one of those links of understanding among the community of strangers.

The state has all these exile colonies—not only old-time Floridians who feel displaced at home but refugees from the Midwest, the Northeast, the

South, and the Caribbean—who have legitimate cause for homesickness.

Looking back, it seems natural that common counterpoint would begin to arise. One striking example came in Florida's splendid array of festivals. The festivals arose in a fever of promotion and celebration of heritage and grew enormously. They had organic ancestry—barn raisings, hog killings, cakewalks, church bazaars, corn shuckings—and evolved into a combination of folk culture and entertainment. Though they did not solve Florida's problems of community, festivals fit perfectly as a part of the solution. They offered native expression that blended an attractive dose of old Florida with community fun. In this quilt of a state the direction was right, at least.

During the 1980s, almost anyone could find a festival they liked and the custom appeared steady for the future. The weekend celebration of life never stopped, rarely paused. From the villages to the cities, more than 600 great public parties spread across the peninsula like so many New England town meetings that had turned into parties. The subject was pleasure, not civics, but about them was a festive nationalism that tried to stitch the state's varied parts together. Some came on the scene only for a year or two and expired; others endured and became part of the folk tradition. Not even the state division of tourism felt it could keep a complete and up-to-date list.

Festivals became Florida's most casual, and perhaps best, stimulus for a statewide community spirit. They made a trail that covered almost every weekend on the calendar, setting up open-air hurrahs for things that Floridians found significiant for both whimsical and serious reasons. One year I toted up an estimate that five million persons a year attended Florida festivals celebrating food, music, art, folklife, history, and whatever else came to mind. The festivals identified and revealed Florida's splendid human variety, its fancies, and even its problems and made positive contributions to them.

At a place called Otter Springs a crowd of 5,000 would gather on July 4 to see who could belly flop off a high-diving board and make the biggest splash. Along the Caloosahatchee River at quaint LaBelle, about 35,000 would come each February to eat the hearts out of the official state tree—the Sabal palm—at the Swamp Cabbage Festival. Naples rolled out the swamp buggies for a happy wallow in the October mud with 8,000 watching. Key West separately celebrated Conch beginnings and on-the-edge culture. The Holmes County village of Ponce de León had a collard greens festival. Wausau chose a possum theme. Niceville defended the honor of its favorite fish, the mullet, with a festival that sometimes drew as many as 100,000. Some, like the Florida Seafood Festival at Apalachicola, grew so popular that town fathers worried whether crowds would be too big to handle. Cedar Key had popular seafood and arts festivals. Macclenny had a Moonshine Festival. Spring Hill had chicken plucking. Palatka celebrated the blooming of the azaleas with a festival.

More celebrated were the Florida Folklife Program, which put together a sample of the whole state's folkways on a May weekend at the Stephen Foster Folk Culture Center in White Springs. Tallahassee contributed Springtime Tallahassee, honoring a special time of the year there. Tampa contributed in major-league style with the Gasparilla Festival in February. Carnaval Miami, celebrating Hispanic heritage, brought out estimates of more than a half million in March. Pompano Beach had Christmas boat parades down the IntraCoastal Waterway. St. Petersburg had a Festival of States; Jacksonville had a Jazz Festival; Pensacola put on a Mardi Gras. Fernandina Beach, Marathon, Everglades City, and Grant joined those having seafood festivals. Fort Myers held the Edison Festival of Light. Sanibel Island honored its seashells, Zellwood its corn, Belle Glade its winter vegetables, McIntosh its Gay '90s ambience.

Festivals conjured up an identifiable Florida spirit, a whiff of the state's essence. They established threads of commonality among the disparate. They offered glimpses of comfortable oneness rather than alienation, and Florida found a way to make a serious contribution out of fun. They established a direction, a way.

Only if judged against itself, by its own standards and not those of some other place with far worse problems, can Florida make intelligent measurements of loss and gain. Without remembering and honoring old Florida and its natural gifts, the state runs the risk of lowered expectations. We would forget how it could be, how it used to be. We would decide that there were no answers to growth except lowered standards and then quit trying. We would expect the traffic to be congested, the water to taste funny, the air to smell bad, the landscape to be measled with commercial blots, the politicians to be slippery if not corrupt. We would risk the inclination to view a declining Florida as inevitable and accept a bad swap: real Florida for a kind of placelessness that could be lifted up and transplanted to almost any other region. With that, we would lose our genuine feel and full appreciation for this distinctive peninsula.

Florida's greatest problem evolves into understanding itself because understanding precedes all answers. In my time, I felt that upon better understanding rested the survival of certain qualities of life that historically have been associated with Florida. The job for the pioneers, for example, was to conquer natural Florida, to tame it, to make it habitable. They did it, maybe too thoroughly. Then the job became to preserve what was left, to blend all the parts and bridge all the gaps and to treat it as a home to be nurtured and prized, not as a rental for which someone else was responsible. It is difficult to understand something that is still defining itself, as Florida is, but without serious understanding there can be no intelligently conceived political will to face Florida's realities, no focused expression from the voters to guide the politicians.

The old environmental warrior, Nat Reed of Hobe Sound, probably said it best: "Just because we have the ability to control the earth does not mean it is in our best interest to do so. . . . When we wound the earth, we wound ourselves."

We need to understand that almost everything we love about Florida is at risk. We need such a clear understanding that we express our love and appreciation in the way that we live. We need to live—and to structure our communities—in ways that make our highest values clear, set compelling standards of behavior, and clearly establish customs others respect. We need to illuminate the thousands of mysteries about Florida so that everyone can know the fascination of learning about them. We need to realize that the great migrating tides of Florida are as wonderful to read as a classic book that you never can finish, one that goes on and on, adding chapter after chapter. We must understand that there is a balance among all those tidal forces and this physical environment that permits us to have the extraordinary advantages of Florida—but only if we pay the cost of being responsible, only if we do our part.

With that, we have a chance not only to save some of what we had but also to create a better Florida—and one, most important, that remains true to itself.

Postscript: My Florida

Sunrise begins everything. Anywhere along the east coast you can see it rise with royal colors out of the Atlantic Ocean. Almost any spot on a palm-framed sand dune, with a fresh breeze moving the heavily salty air, could make Methuselah feel young and imaginative.

By the clock or by the calendar, Florida changes and reflects and reveals competing new wonders every day. Cautious Crackers do not like to choose one favorite thing. It is like asking a daddy to name his favorite child. All of them are favorites, including the next one. Ask instead to match a choice vista to a time of day, or a mood to a place, or an appetite to a month of the year. Pin the fancy of the moment to any one of a hundred places on the Florida map—South Florida in winter, for example, or North Florida in spring, in truth all Florida most of the time.

One favorite sunrise came at St. Paul's Episcopal Church along Duval Street in Key West, where the mood is the thing, not the colors; there is no clear view of the colors. By special dispensation, in Key West you are permitted to celebrate sunrise at nine, for even that is radically early for Duval Street. One Wednesday morning, 1985, it was so quiet inside the chapel that even tentative footsteps echoed off the high ceilings during quiet prayers, providing in the half-light a memorably different version of sunrise.

The Bohemian-bent Key West of fable prefers reveille come just in time for the sunset, and please not a bugled beginning. It likes to start the day with something gently insistent to arouse the mind. Squabbling pelicans and gulls do nicely.

During the night Key West, where nearly all human appetites have a choice, makes a lot of noise. Glitz rises and pops all around in bright little neon-eyed oases. The street shifts into higher and higher gears, finally cresting and winding down, exhausted as the sunrise strikes. For a little while, it gives us a drowsily different city. The pulse of Duval Street slows to a sleeper's rhythms. The fabled Key West of the night hides out. A morning Key West enjoys its time.

The heavy doors of St. Paul's, the historic Cathedral of the Keys and the only church on Duval Street, swung open two and one-half hours earlier. Someone off the street might have been sleeping out there in the churchyard under the poinciana tree, among the hibiscus and oleanders and frangipani and crotons. It does not interfere. With morning, the church welcomes you, one and all.

From the street go up a half-dozen steps, and you have arrived at a place much higher than the altitude of 10 feet suggests. Outside, Duval Street rests fretfully; inside, serenity rules. Walk across the huge tiles, listening to the echoes. Stare up at the bewitchingly deep colors of the stained-glass windows that depict a bald St. Paul.

Some of the faithful have gathered. The tall windows have been pivoted open, too. A fan hums. The candles flicker. Feel the ethereal cool. Smell the sweat and flower blossoms on the breeze, a mix of human and heavenly scent.

Nine sit or kneel in that southeast corner of the cathedral called Lady Chapel. A tenth trots in late, puffing. All but one have gray hair. The Rev. Norbert Cooper, a Bahamian, a visiting celebrant from St. Peter's across town, enters in long white vestments. His strong, faintly accented voice rolls around the rafters impressively as he recites beautiful words from the Book of Common Prayer.

The 10 go to the iron rail and kneel, each taking from Father Cooper a wafer of altar bread that has been shaped by the women of St. Paul's on a handpress, each sipping wine from a common cup, a golden chalice.

Outside, a tourist trolley trundles down Duval Street. The worshipers can hear the loudspeaker, a voice from the world, explaining St. Paul's, though not very well. In the pews, the 10 "pass the peace"—shaking hands with the strangers near them, wishing them well. That soothing blessing comes in Father Cooper's pronouncement: "The Peace of the Lord Be with You Always."

The 10 go their way back out onto Duval Street, where passersby look at them curiously. A forlorn looking man sits on the waist-high wall bordering the sidewalk. Already, he waits for the night.

In Key West, the morning experience at St. Paul's might not be true sunrise, except in the mind, but it is both historic and symbolic.

One hundred fifty-four years earlier, while Andrew Jackson was President and Key West land sold for $25 an acre, the town council decided there should be something more than makeshift religious services at the courthouse. A letter went to the Episcopal bishop in New York requesting a priest.

The letter assured the bishop that the priest would have "little to apprehend" in Key West. It sweetened the prospects by adding that the new man would not be required to stay in town during August and September; but priests were hard to keep. By the time Mrs. John W. C. Fleming had given land on Duval Street for a church and the coral rock structure had been completed in 1839, the fourth priest was in residence.

Buildings were hard to keep, too. In 1846, a hurricane blew the church down. The parishioners replaced it with a frame building. That burned in 1884. Another wooden church replaced it. Another hurricane blew that one down in 1909. They built the present St. Paul's, the fourth, out of concrete, and it lasts as an extraordinary haven on a unique street full of searchers and dreamers and in-betweeners.

Neither hurricanes nor fires nor glitz have extinguished this church. They simply enlarge the market. The morning people and the night people stand cheek to cheek on a tight little island, and St. Paul's still prays. It makes a beautiful sunrise, of a sort.

There are so many lovely sunrises, ways to start the day, in Florida. For me, it is hard to beat the one that rises over our little lake, a visually changeable feast that varies as the sun moves with the calendar. This one suits our peculiarities best. If we are not awake, it gently beams into the windows and announces the time. If we beat the sun up, coffee by the gazebo and maybe an early morning swim for Gloria, which puts ripples into those reflected colors, deliver the day to us as though it came by special delivery from heaven.

In my memory, though, probably no sunrise—in a public place—ever quite matched the one at the wildlife sanctuary on Sanibel Island. There, the sun rises classically out of tidal flats and mangroves, and creatures come alive as the rays reach them. The birds wake up first. Brown pelicans of ancient and awkward design slap flat-footedly at the water as they struggle to take flight, becoming modernly sleek and graceful once they lift off. Black skimmers plow the water, their beaks cutting a small wake as they fly low and scoop up breakfast on the run. Long-legged, beautifully pink roseate spoonbills stroll elegantly about in shallow water, sensitive Cyranos that make poetry for the eyes despite noses that could turn pancakes. Little brown rabbits hop along the side of the road under the watchful eyes of red-shouldered hawks and ospreys. Alligators silently poke long snouts out of the water to see the menu. After a morning splash, anhingas spread their wings for drying, while herons and ibises move across the horizon against the backdrop of a bloodied-orange sun.

❦ My best day in Florida, or yours, could begin in a thousand ways, all of them special. An early morning coffee in Tallahassee is nice, staring up the street at that beloved old capitol; the awesome newer one rises behind it like King Kong after a full-length shave and whitewash. Or maybe you could take your doughnut and stand on the bulkheads below the Sunshine Skyway between St. Petersburg and Sarasota and watch the fishermen wading out to surf-cast while ships entering Tampa Bay make gentle waves.

You could take your fixings and stroll the bulkheads approaching the Castillo de San Marcos in St. Augustine and catch that fresh breeze as it sweeps across the oldest city, or grab one of those fabulous fried mullet breakfasts at Cedar Key, or climb atop the big dike where it circles past Pahokee and stare across huge Lake Okeechobee and eat a granola bar while wondering at all the water it holds for thirsty South Florida. Or, eat an orange on the Indian River, or go behind restaurant glass at Fort Lauderdale and eat your eggs while watching the beautiful people stretch and yawn and amble goldenly out on the beach. The possibilities stretch out, with lunch and dinner still to go.

Enjoying your best day in Florida requires being in several places at once. As the sun climbs, we might go driving in the Panhandle: take U.S. 98 along the coast through Apalachicola and Mexico Beach and Panama City and Destin all the way to Pensacola and see old and new Florida all at once. Loop up U.S. 29 to Century and swing back below the borders of Alabama and Georgia, and see Florida's Southern connection, across which the old Crackers flowed with wagons and mules to grab for a piece of Florida during the Boom. Drive U.S. 90 east toward Tallahassee, Florida's equivalent of a mountain drive, through DeFuniak Springs and Chipley.

For lunch, how about a cruise down the St. Johns River from Jacksonville, the river city with one of Florida's most impressive skylines? Go behind the seven-brick-thick walls at the old Palace Saloon in Fernandina Beach and eat boiled shrimp while listening to a player piano, or try the famed Columbia Restaurant in Tampa's Ybor City (and in St. Augustine, too), where they still serve Spanish-style banquets that would inflate a blimp. Try Riverview Charlie's in New Smyrna Beach, where you can pop a boiled shrimp and occasionally watch the porpoises at play. Eat apple pie in Dunnellon. In season, trek on down to Everglades City and wolf down succulent stone crabs while sitting at a cement table. Go to Little Havana for *carne asado con frijoles negroes y arroz*.

During the siesta hour, one choice dominates, the most serene public place in Florida—the beautiful Bok Tower gardens atop Iron Mountain near Lake Wales, where the sounds of a carillon housed in the tower of a mini–Taj Mahal enchantingly sound across the landscape. A wealthy old Dutchman, Edward V. Bok, for 30 years a nationally known magazine editor, created the sanctuary during the 1920s because he thought the world needed a beautiful, quiet place.

Spend the afternoon walking the pink-orange sands at Flagler Beach, where you can pad on down to Daytona Beach, if you wish. Boat on the Suwannee or Santa Fe rivers; experience one of Florida's finest treats by tubing down the clear, cold Ichetucknee River. Catch a bass in Lake George. Play shuffleboard at Mount Dora. Go for a spin along the oceanfront in Palm Beach, where all that glitters truly might be gold. Ride down U.S. 27 through the orange groves atop Florida's great ridge. Put a canoe into a spring-fed river in the Ocala National Forest. Join the gawking tourists for a sample of the past-that-never-was at Disney World. Fly over the great ranches and prairies in the southwest. Ride into cattle country and see the Florida cowboys, from Kissimmee and St. Cloud down to Wauchula and back over to Fort Pierce. Take an airboat through the sawgrass and big-sky horizons of the Everglades. Boat down the St. Lucie River. Ride across the big bridge with the great view at Sebastian Inlet. Visit Cape Canaveral for a space shot, and feel the earth rumble and the sky light up. Marvel at the desolation around Mulberry, Polk County's dusty phosphate capital. In every corner of Florida, something special awaits.

For sunset, go back down to the docks at Key West and let the daylight hours end in the city where they began. Join the crowd for the intriguingly bizarre volunteer show, and applaud as the sun goes down. You won't have any trouble being sincere about it.

For a celebratory dinner, in Key West there is Louie's Backyard and several others. Many favor Bern's Restaurant in Tampa as the special place, but there are dozens of other elegant spots along both the Gold and Gulf coasts. For evening, I like nostalgia and my easy chair at home, but if you are the restless type you might like to tour the Church Street Station complex in downtown Orlando or brave the old boardwalk at Daytona Beach or test the carnival at Panama City during the summer season.

❨ I have been lucky. Newspapermen rarely have the chance to work with as many choices of subject and location and approach as I did. Many of them must do their thinking and their composing while under the strains of a competitive sprint as clock-watching editors fret. As a result, they must learn to do some things fast and almost reflexively. As long as you are cloistered in the office where there are shared appreciations, all of it seems quite grand and significant and sometimes even heroic, and sometimes it might be. Once you go outside the cloister, though, the insulation of the newsroom wears off, and in time you discover in realistic ways that the world views the role of the press with great skepticism. Most of the pragmatic folk I encountered tended to regard the First Amendment to the U.S. Constitution (guaranteeing a free press) as a granted right for the common good, not an open-ended immunity or exemption that ripples off into a kind of 007 license that assures no accountability. They tended to see news people as subject to the same human standards and values, the same requirements for courtesy in human relations, and responsibility in community affairs as everyone else. Even among good and honest and intelligent folk, as a newsman I generated a little bit of fear and skepticism unless I was able to persuade them that I understood and accepted those common burdens. The effect on me gradually was to re-form my character, at least on this issue, to make me more aware and appreciative of the need for civility in public affairs and for compassion in personal ones, more sensitive to the reasons there need to be United Ways and chambers of commerce and churches and civic organizations that target unusual human needs. Out of the cloister, things looked different. That affected the way I saw Florida, too.

❡ All of us who live in the state have our own Florida. It is a personal matter. If my private tastes range from pompano to mullet, from kum-quats to peaches, from spoon bread to croissants to corn bread, from black-eyed peas to kiwi to snails—and yours cannot stomach some of those things—without tolerance and courtesy we might never be able to dine together in peace. Consider my Florida, offered without prejudice to yours. In two decades of traveling the state, my tastes evolved.

Looking back, the little things rise in importance as memories: the blessing of good neighbors, pockets of nature forgotten and flourishing, porpoises leaping free of the ocean between me and the beach, an alliga-tor in heat bellowing and thrashing in the lake just off our yard, an eagle classically swooping down near our dock to clutch at duck decoys, deer feeding in the yard, a succession of dogs—Lancer, Lady, and Brownie—enriching our lives with good humor and loyalty, flashes of free Cracker spirit and wisdom that defied easy classification.

I remember well the many visits to the free city of Cedar Key, a place that fended for itself and liked it that way. I had a long history with Cedar Key, first visiting that Gulf Coast fishing village when I was two weeks old. No memory typified the place for me better than the time I visited there in 1984 and they told me down at city hall that the city had acquired a traffic light. An admirer who lived in Central Florida, whose hometown had bought some new traffic lights, sent one of the older ones to Cedar Key. The gift was graciously accepted—and stored in the fire-house. Ce-dar Key at that time did not care for such trappings of urban madness.

A Panhandle hog killing ranks high, too. At the invitation of the Flach family, one bright winter morning we went up to their farm north of Bonifay, near the Alabama line, and joined in the festive event. Little about the nasty but fascinating affair has been forgotten.

Not long after dawn, on a day so cold that Rudolf Flach's breath fogged, he knelt in the dirt beneath his backyard live oak tree and shot a frightened, squealing hog named Wilbur in the forehead with a .22 rifle. Wilbur fell over on his side, convulsing, kicking up little puffs of dust. Flach and his wife, Carol, dragged the carcass to a hoist hanging from an oak limb and hauled it up by the heels until it swung free in air that smelled of woodsmoke. With a long butcher knife, Rudy slit Wilbur's throat and, as the blood poured out, Carol thrust a tin kitchen pot underneath and caught six pounds of it. That was how the all-day affair started. The Flachs turned the necessary slaughter into a celebration. They invited the neighbors over for that unforgettable day in 1980, our first hog killing in Florida.

Never will we forget the yodel of the sandhill cranes as they echoed across the ancient dune hills near our home. The cranes fly in an aerial string that gently waves as the cranes trail across the sky gobbling melodically. Their song, the Snowbird gobble, becomes the strains of the Florida winter and will turn your head every time.

The sandhill crane became my favorite bird. The cranes are both migratory and resident, well representative of Florida. In a state whose pulse develops out of a pattern of movements—the warming sweep of the Gulf stream, the rising and falling tides, the seasonal migrations of birds and fishes and people—the cranes fit with beautiful symbolism. Like Crackers and Snowbirds, they should not be mistaken as only simple, dumb creatures. They have many curls and depths. The cranes' strange song, which some hear as a yodel and some as a turkeylike gobble, is distinctive because it comes out of a unique instrument—a windpipe that loops as it makes its way through a long neck, producing that gobbling or gargling effect. Their call blankets the landscape more completely and distinctly than any other unaided sound from a single living thing. Delivered from a quarter mile up in the air, it reverberates across hills and prairies and swamp flats for miles around.

Beyond that, cranes dance better (and more continuously) and feather out with more of the elegantly careless Florida style than any other bird. The crane, a red crown slung over its eyes like a beret, has a commanding presence. It stands about four feet tall, grayishly feathered and plump in the middle, with a seven-foot wingspread. If it wore dark glasses and a gaudy shirt, the guise would be perfect.

It became an annual winter ritual for us to visit a North Florida pasture not far from where we live, a place where a couple of hundred cranes usually winter in privacy, and watch them doing their famous dance. The movements resemble a fat man's ballet, awkward and labored, as long as they are on the ground. When the cranes whirl their wings, as though suddenly inspired to rise above their limitations, they are lifted into the air with a grace that the earthbound simply cannot muster.

Cranes don't have those classic Florida roots, but that's okay. Most Floridians today don't have the roots, either. What cranes have is rhythm, and in this peculiar state rhythm is more permanent than roots.

¶ All those special memories, and many more, round out the picture of Florida in our time. Probably none had more lasting impact than an experiment in retirement on Miami Beach. For one month in 1980, Gloria and I tried living in a small apartment in South Beach on an income of $700 a month. The assignment for *Tropic Magazine* started as a lark and became a serious experiment.

During our first days we met a veteran of the retirement scene on a park bench, confessing we were rookies who did not know how to handle this abrupt change, and he gave us some good advice. "It takes a while," he said. "Do not give up too much too fast. Save what you can of the old life. See what will fit, and keep it. You must remember that you have not become new people. . . . Old age doesn't change you. It limits you. Everything goes on. But you can't have any fun if you are a sissy about being old. You cannot begin by deciding that you have been defeated."

We never received better retirement advice, not even after we retired for real. That month helped us better understand that the old want to be loved and sustained by the young, yet the key to that lies in the elderly's own ability to bear the pressures of age so well that the young are sustained by the example. When the desperation of the aged breaks into the open, it becomes a curse to all. The young are repelled by it, for their brains are not wrinkled enough to know better. We learned in real ways that retirement does not mean the end of the fight; it does not mean ease and serenity unless you are brave. The fight just shifts to new ground and new rules. We get that reward of serenity only if we earn it. The terrors— of physical infirmity, loneliness, despair, senility, death—are inevitable. The test is how we deal with whatever number of those that become our lot.

℘ Although I always wanted to have access to a city and all its conveniences, the small towns of Florida became my favorites. Human dimensions there come under easier examination and into clearer focus. Small towns make it easier to appreciate the comedy of the human struggle, the posturing of the players, the sharing of place and dependence. The cities don't need another observer or commentator anyway. They already are explored in great detail and lauded as the center of the universe. In the small towns, we get a knothole view of them, and the distant angle refreshes.

A state with 20,000 lakes and 1,700 streams and countless natural springs (17 of them major), with 1,300 miles of coastline and a climate that ranges from temperate to subtropical, has a thousand or more places that could qualify as a favorite. There are islands, swamps, beaches, highlands. There are urban canyons and rural pastures. There is a place to fit your dreams, your mood, your pocketbook, your taste. You can create your own personal Florida.

My Florida never was the one in which tourists go seeking a tan and find a sunburn. My Florida learned long ago to live with the sun by seeking shade under a tree, not a cabana. My Florida might not be yours, but I am happy to share it with you anyway.

Bibliography

Akin, Edward N. *Flagler: Rockefeller Partner and Florida Baron.* Gainesville: University Press of Florida, 1988.

Arana, Luis Rafael, and Albert Manucy. *The Building of Castillo de San Marcos.* Eastern National Park and Monument Association for Castillo de San Marcos National Monument, 1977.

Bigelow, Gordon E. *Frontier Eden: The Literary Career of Marjorie Kinnan Rawlings.* Gainesville: University Press of Florida, 1966.

Bigelow, Gordon E., and Laura V. Monti, eds. *Selected Letters of Marjorie Kinnan Rawlings.* Gainesville: University Press of Florida, 1983.

Bosselman, Fred P. *In the Wake of the Tourist.* Washington, D.C.: The Conservation Foundation, 1978.

Burt, Al. Articles and columns in *The Miami Herald* (including *Tropic Magazine*) from 1973 to 1996.

———. *Becalmed in the Mullet Latitudes.* Port Salerno, Fla.: Florida Classics Library, 1984.

Burt, Al, and Heinz Erhardt. *Florida: A Place in the Sun.* Offenburg, West Germany: Burda GmbH, 1974.

Carr, Archie. *A Naturalist in Florida: A Celebration of Eden.* Edited by Marjorie Carr. New Haven, Conn.: Yale University Press, 1994.

———. *Ulendo: Travels of a Naturalist In and Out of Africa.* New York: Knopf, 1964; Gainesville: University Press of Florida, 1993.

———. *The Windward Road: Adventures of a Naturalist on Remote Caribbean Shores.* New York: Knopf, 1955; Tallahassee: Florida State University Press, 1979.

DeGrove, John M. *Land, Growth, and Politics.* Washington, D.C.: Planners Press, 1984.

Douglas, Marjory Stoneman. *The Everglades: River of Grass.* Coconut Grove, Fla.: Hurricane House Publishers, 1947.

———. *Florida: The Long Frontier.* New York: Harper & Row, 1967.

Federal Writers' Project of the Works Project Administration for the State of Florida. *Florida: A Guide to the Southernmost State.* New York: Oxford University Press, 1939.

Gannon, Michael. *Florida: A Short History.* Gainesville: University Press of Florida, 1993.

Graham, Thomas. *The Awakening of St. Augustine: The Anderson Family and the Oldest City.* St. Augustine: St. Augustine Historical Society, 1978.

Hanna, A. J., and Kathryn Abbey Hanna. *Lake Okeechobee.* Indianapolis and New York: Bobbs-Merrill Co., 1948.

Howard, Kennie L. *Yesterday in Florida.* New York: Carlton Press, 1970.

Johnson, Malcolm B. *Red, White, and Bluebloods.* Tallahassee, Fla.: Rotary Clubs of Tallahassee, 1976.

———. *I Declare!* Tallahassee, Fla.: *Tallahassee Democrat,* 1983.

Kennedy, Stetson. *Palmetto Country.* New York: Duell, Sloan & Pearce, 1942. Reprint, Gainesville: University Press of Florida, 1989.

Lanier, Sidney. *Florida: Its Scenery, Climate, and History.* Facsimile ed. Gainesville: University Press of Florida, 1973.

Laurie, Murray D., comp. *Melrose Architectural and Historical Survey.* Melrose, Fla.: Historic Melrose, Inc., 1988.

Lyons, Ernest. *The Last Cracker Barrel.* New York: Newspaper Enterprise Association, 1973.

———. *My Florida.* New York: A. S. Barnes & Co., 1969.

Morris, Allen. *The Florida Handbook.* Tallahassee, Fla.: Peninsular Publishing Co., biennial editions from 1973 to 1996.

Rawlings, Marjorie Kinnan. *Cross Creek.* New York: Grosset & Dunlap, 1942.

Smith, Pat. *Forever Island.* New York: W. P. Norton & Co., 1973.

———. *A Land Remembered.* Sarasota: Pineapple Press, 1983.

Strickland, Nadine. *Cracker Girl.* Gainesville: Florida Living Magazine, 1994.

Tebeau, Charlton. *A History of Florida,* rev. ed. Coral Gables, Fla.: University of Miami Press, 1980.

Tolles, Zonira Hunter. *Shadows on the Sand.* Keystone Heights, Fla.: Zonira Hunter Tolles, 1976.

———. *Bonnie Melrose.* Keystone Heights, Fla.: Zonira Hunter Tolles, 1982.

Waterbury, Jean Parker, ed. *The Oldest City: St. Augustine, Saga of Survival.* St. Augustine, Fla.: St. Augustine Historical Society, 1983.

Wright, J. Leitch. *British St. Augustine.* St. Augustine, Fla.: Historic St. Augustine Preservation Board, 1975.

Index

Pasco County, 22
Paul, Carlton, 150
Paul, Maureen, 149
Pearce, Bill, 132
Pennekamp, John, 48, 56, 63, 131–34. *See also* photo section
Penney Farms, 100
Penney, J. C., 100
Pensacola, 8, 13, 22, 38, 77, 78, 84, 97, 98, 112–14, 155, 162, 169
Pine Level, 22
Polk County, 43, 85
Pompano Beach, 162
Poppell, Pat, 150
Port Mayaca, 105
Port St. Joe, 98, 99
Punta Rassa, 85, 87

Quillian, Irene, 131

Rains, Faye, 126–28
Raulerson, Annie, 85, 87
Raulerson, Hiram, 85–88. *See also* photo section
Raulerson, Lewis, 87
Raulerson, Noel, 85
Raulerson, Peter, 85–87. *See also* photo section
Rawlings, Marjorie Kinnan, 106–8, 148
Reed, Nathaniel Pryor, 48, 117–19, 163
Reno, Janet, 158
Renzelman, Peg, 150
Rices, the, 150
Richards, Capt. Thomas E., 45, 46
Roast Ear, 72
Rogers, Gamble, 19, 121–23. *See also* photo section
Rowell, E. C., 12
Ruhl, Dan, 43
Runnels, Davage J., Jr., 38–39
Russell, Benjamin, 62

Russell, Bernard, 73–75
Russell, David, 62
Rutland, Clarence, 22. *See also* photo section
Rynds, the, 150

San Agustin Antiguo,, 94, 95
Sanford, 47, 97
Sanibel, 8, 22, 61, 85, 162, 168. *See also* photo section
Sarasota, 67, 75, 168
Sebastian Inlet, 170
Sebring, Billy, 100
Sebring, George A., 100
Sebring, 8, 42, 100, 102
Sholtz, Gov. David, 11
Sikes, Robert, 32
Simkins, Bob, 150
Simpsons, the, 146
Slazor, Esther, 150
Smiley, Nixon, 109
Smith, Elizabeth, 130, 131
Smith, Pat, 109
Spratt, Edna, 150
Spring Hill, 162
St. Augustine, 8, 84, 92–98, 114–17, 123, 144, 145, 168, 169, 175, 176. *See also* photo section
St. Augustine Historical Society, 92, 93, 175
St. Cloud, 170
St. Johns River, 35, 97, 144, 145, 169
St. Lucie River, 118, 170
St. Marys River, 35, 37
St. Petersburg, 72, 106, 162, 168
Stegall children, 149
Steinhatchee, 72
Stone, Jesse, 99
Stone, T. H., 99
Stuart, 129, 157
Summerlin, Jacob, 102

Suwannee River, 42, 127
Swearingen, Mary Lou and John, 143, 146

Tallahassee, 8–13, 17, 39, 51, 77, 97, 98, 115, 124, 130, 144, 155, 162, 168, 169, 175, 176
Tampa Bay, 33, 75, 97, 155, 168
Thomson, Edith, 150
Thomson, Phil, 150
Titus, Col. Harry, 100
Titusville, 44, 47, 100
Tolles, Zonira Hunter, 144
Traceys, the, 146
Trueblood, Felicity, 146
Trumbull, Steve, 10
Tschinkel, Victoria J., 67
Twine, Henry L., 114–17

Umatilla, 119
Umbrella Key, 62
University of FLorida, 5, 21, 95, 107, 109, 119, 120, 137, 145, 146, 155, 175

Van Giesen, Bob, 150
Vero Beach, 18, 50, 108

Wakulla County, 130

Wakulla Springs, 39, 40, 42, 61. *See also* photo section
Waldo, 144
Walker, Frank, 35, 36
Wall, Amber and Martha, 146
Walton County, 31, 32, 38
Warner, the Rev. Dale, 150, 151
Warner, Lempi, 150
Warren, Gov. Fuller, 36
Warren, Kathi, 149
Washington, Ray, 109
Wauchula, 170
West Palm Beach, 16, 50, 52, 155
Whidden, Tempa, 85
White Springs, 47, 122, 162
Will, Lawrence, 87, 105–6
Williams, Don, 148
Williams, Reda and Don, 146
Willmore, Mabel Richards, 45
Windley Key, 56, 62, 64, 73. *See also* photo section
Winter Park, 72, 123
Wodraska, John, 118

Ybor City, 169
Yulee, David, 37

Zellwood, 162